I am convinced that God created the home to be a workshop in which Christian character can be built. What an opportunity God has given us!

O Israel, listen: Jehovah is our God, Jehovah alone. You must love him with all your heart, soul, and might. And you must think constantly about these commandments I am giving you today.
You must teach them to your children and talk about them when you are at home or out for a walk; at bedtime and the first thing in the morning.
Deuteronomy 6:4-7, TLB

Good Times for Your Family

Wayne E. Rickerson

G/L
REGAL
BOOKS
™

A Division of G/L Publications
Glendale, California, U.S.A.

To my wife Janet and my girls
Heidi, Liesl and Bridget
with whom I have had many good times.

Scripture quotations are designated . . .
NASB, New American Standard Bible. ©The Lockman
Foundation, 1971. Used by permission.
TLB, The Living Bible.© Tyndale House, 1971. Used
by permission.
Phillips, The New Testament in Modern English.
©J.B. Phillips, 1958. Used by permission of Macmillan Company.

The Authorized King James Version is the basic text.

Published by Family Life Library
Regal Books Division, G/L Publications
Glendale, California 91209, U.S.A.

Library of Congress Catalog No. 76-3934

ISBN 0-8307-0427-2

Contents

Good Times Are Important!

Do you know how important good times with the family are for your children?

True, your youngsters are not apt to run up to you and say, "Hey, Mom and Dad, we need more family time!" But children do have a deep need for meaningful good times with their parents.

This is especially true when it comes to children learning and understanding Christian values.

I am convinced that God created the home to be a workshop in which Christian character could be built. As early as Genesis God said of Abraham: *For I have chosen him,* (Abraham) *in order that he may command his children and his household after him to keep the way of the Lord* (Gen. 18:19, *NASB*). And even today the home remains the primary place where Christian values can be taught.

As I work with my own family I find that the key to communicating Christian values to our children is *time*. We must spend time with our youngsters if we expect them to know, understand and accept our values. Each week a parent's calendar should include three dimensions of family time: times together around God's Word; just for fun family times; and time spent with each child alone.

My conviction about the importance of spending good family times together is the reason for this book. The first chapter deals with God's plan for home-centered teaching of His Word. The remaining chapters give specific, practical ideas for Bible sharing, Bible learning family activities. When you can do fun things at home with your children and teach them Christian values at the same time, then you have a real winner!

What an opportunity God has given us! There are good times ahead for any family who will share together from God's Word.

Wayne Rickerson

PART

1

God's Plan for Communicating Biblical Values

In a recent cross country survey,[1] Christian families were asked: What kind of help do you feel your family needs?

When the results were tabulated, *teaching children Christian values* was one of the three top areas of concern. How can Christian parents effectively communicate biblical values? Can parents help children accept God's love and His way? Does Scripture give any clues?

The first three chapters of *Good Times for Your Family* focus on what the Bible has to say about these questions.

---

1. The survey questionnaires were answered by over 1000 parents attending *International Center of Learning* seminars held in cities across the United States. The questionnaires were prepared by the Family Life Division of G/L Publications.

chapter 1

God Wants Parents to Teach

If you could look in on some of our family together times you might wonder just what is going on.

Maybe you would find Liesl and Bridget making their own "joyful noise" to the Lord as they happily "play" metal mixing bowls with tablespoons while the rest of us clap and sing.

Or, you might discover all of us acting out a happening in the life of our Lord. For example, one night Heidi bandaged one of her legs so that she had to hobble into the room on crutches. Then we pantomimed one of Jesus' healing miracles.

On other evenings you would find all of us busy making posters showing a biblical principle at work in everyday life. One evening, when we talked about Jesus wanting us to be kind to one another, Liesl made a "helping others" poster with pictures of helping situations that she had cut from a magazine.

Why do we feel all of this is so important?

Scripture makes it clear that God wants parents to teach His ways and His values in the family circle. To the parents of Israel's families God said:

And these words, which I am commanding you today, shall be on your heart; and you shall teach them diligently to your sons and shall talk of them when you sit in your house and when you walk by the way and when you lie down and when you rise up (Deut. 6:6,7, *NASB*).

Jesus showed His love and concern for children when some youngsters were brought to Him and the disciples tried to send them away. *Let the children alone*, He said, *and do not hinder them from coming to Me* (Matt. 19:14, *NASB*).

The apostle Paul spoke directly to parents. *Do not provoke your children to anger; but bring them up in the discipline and instruction of the Lord* (Eph. 6:4, *NASB*). Or as another version puts it: *Bring them up in the nurture and admonition of the Lord* (Eph. 6:4).

As Christian parents we need to plan for ways our homes can become "nurture centers" for our children. God wants parents to pass on to each of their children their own faith and experiences of God's love and care.

Who is to teach? Both parents are to teach. The father and mother are to be a teaching team, but the Scriptures give the dad the responsibility of lead teacher. From the beginning the Bible depicts the father as the family's spiritual leader, responsible for communicating God's Word and for the building of family unity.

It was the Hebrew father's assigned responsibility to pass on to his son his experiences of God's love and care. The sons would then teach their sons, and so generation after generation would be taught God's Word. As Deuteronomy 4:9,10 says: *Only give heed to yourself and keep your soul*

*diligently lest you forget the things which your eyes have seen,
and lest they depart from your heart all the days of your life;
but make them known to your sons and your grandsons . . .
that I may let them hear My words so they may learn to fear
Me all the days they live on the earth, and that they may teach
their children (NASB).*

The New Testament re-emphasizes the father's responsibility to teach his children. The apostle Paul, in Ephesians
says, *Fathers, don't overcorrect your children or make it
difficult for them to obey the commandment. Bring them up
with Christian teaching in Christian discipline* (Eph. 6:4,
Phillips).

Secular studies now tell us what God has said all along,
that a good father is extremely important in the healthy
emotional, intellectual and spiritual development of children
in a stable family life.

As I read Deuteronomy 6:4-9, I see it talking about three
basic teaching principles that are needed for a teaching/
nurturing life-style.

Modeling—Teaching by Example

God's instruction to parents begins with a challenge for
their commitment to Him:

*Love the Lord your God with all your heart and with all your
soul and with all your might* (Deut. 6:5, *NASB*).

Personal commitment—this is the key to being an effective
Christian model and example in the home. As Larry
Richards says in his thought-provoking book on home-
centered Christian education: "It is a basic principle of
human life that we communicate what is in our hearts to our
children, for good or for bad.

"Sociologists speak much of the processes by which what
is in the heart—the core of the personality—is transmitted to

18

others. The processes by which likeness is communicated are most often spoken of as 'modeling' or 'identification.'

"Wherever there is close emotional involvement as in the parent-child relationship, there will be modeling and identification. . . . Strikingly, identification is a process that focuses on what we *are*, not what we *say*.

"This is why God has given us the great prerequisite, His great warning: '*These words . . . shall be on your heart.*' Before we can lead our children to love and obey God, we ourselves must be loving and obeying Him."[1]

Identification is weakened and sometimes destroyed when the parent does not fill his child's need for time and loving attention. If the parent does spend time with his children— playing with them, talking to them, reading to them, doing the things they like to do—identification will be strong and teaching effective.

Time is an expression of love that children can measure. A child thinks, "My parents must really love me. I must be important because they spend time with me." Time spent with children builds that special kind of parent-child relationship upon which identification flourishes.

The identification process is assumed in the Bible. Paul says: *As children copy their fathers you, as God's children, are to copy him* (Eph. 5:1, *Phillips*). This verse makes me nervous, as does all talk about modeling and being an example to my children.

Recently, I heard our three girls screaming at one another in the bedroom. I stomped in and shouted, "Would you girls stop screaming at each other! That's no way to handle things!"

They just stared at me with puzzled looks that said, "What are you talking about, Dad. That's the way you handle things."

There it was in living color. My children identifying with my actions, not my words. Once more, I had to ask God to "change my children's father!" And, in the same breath, to thank Him for His provision for forgiveness. Again I asked for help in communicating God's love and His way to our children—by my life as well as my words.

Teaching by example may seem to be an impossible task. However, God does not ask us to be *perfect* examples. Larry Richards puts it very well when he says: "I am never to communicate perfection to my children or even attempt to! The Bible says that we all sin, and that failure to recognize and admit sins, and confess them to the Lord breaks our fellowship with Him. The same passage suggests that we are to live with others just as we live with God—openly, honestly, confessing, relying on forgiveness and loving to maintain relationship (see Eph. 4:25-32). So, we can be effective Christian parents, *if we are growing Christians,* and if we let our children see us, not as perfect, but as *seeking to grow.*"[2]

Teach Diligently—Formal Teaching

I find in Deuteronomy 6 specific instructions to *teach* our children God's Word: *And these words . . . you shall teach them diligently to your sons* (Deut. 6:6,7, *NASB*). This says to me that God wants parents to have some definite plan for communicating His teachings to the children of the family.

Children need to see that their parents·value His Word enough to share it with them regularly. Through regular family times around God's Word, children become acquainted with God, who He is, what He says, what He has done, what He is doing. Such teaching situations provide opportunities for children to discover that their parents' values are deeply rooted in Scripture.

When "teaching diligently" times are warm experiences of

• Think specifically about *today*. What opportunities did we use? What ones did we miss?

Why Does God Want Parents to Model, Teach, Talk?

There are good reasons why God chose the home as an important place for the teaching and learning of His truth.

• When we teach God's Word at home it becomes obvious to us that our actions must match our words or very little learning will take place. Therefore we must start with ourselves.

• If we are to teach our children well, we must be able to talk about our faith. This causes us to study and apply God's Word.

• As we spend time and teach our children we become better acquainted with their real needs.

• We know and love our children as no one else possibly can. This allows us to understand and touch sensitive areas of our children's lives.

• The home is where the action is! The very best teaching is life-linked. We can teach in real life situations.

• Teaching at home increases communication at the deepest level—at the spiritual level.

When we teach at home, our children have everyday opportunities to know that Christianity is our way of life. As we teach from day-to-day situations we help our children discover that God is involved in everything we do.

Footnotes

1. Lawrence O. Richards, *You, the Parent.* (Chicago: Moody Press, 1974) pp. 19,20.
2. Richards, *You, the Parent*, p. 24.

chapter 2

Guides for Good Family Times

"What do you think makes a happy family?"

That is the question 1,500 school children were asked. And what was the most frequent answer? *Doing things together.* Commenting on the children's response, Marion Leach Jacobsen says, "It's not so much what we do *for* our children that makes fun at home, as what we do *with* them."[1]

And that is the key to having good family together times—*doing things together.* It is the happy, warm feeling of doing things *with* each other that makes a family time a good time.

Seven Basics for Good Family Times

As we have shared family together times at our house during the past three years we have discovered some basic guides that help us have good times together. Here are seven suggestions to help you make your family together times successful.

Choose a time that is right for your family. Family schedules vary, but most families are together certain times each day. Use one of these times for a few minutes of family sharing and Bible learning. At our house, we find the time following dinner is good for our family.

Variety. You must approach God's Word in new and interesting ways if family times are to be successful. Use the over 100 activities suggested in Chapters 3-12 of this book as idea starters. Also, use your own creativity as you adapt the suggestions and think of ways to study God's Word that will be interesting to your family.

In her book, *Honey for a Child's Heart*, Gladys Hunt tells of an interesting Bible study method her husband used at their family times. They would read through a short Bible passage and then each person would ask a question and answer a question.

At first when the children were young, the questions were simple, fact questions. However, as the children grew older, they asked thought questions such as: "Why did Jesus say that?" and, "What does He mean?" and, "What can we learn from what Jesus said?"[2]

The kinds of Bible learning activities you use will depend on the ages and interests of your children. Preschool-age children enjoy simple stories from a Bible storybook. Add variety by asking questions, drawing pictures of the stories and talking about the pictures. Little ones also like the fun of acting out the Bible stories. As your children grow older you will discover a wide range of reading material and activities for your family together times.

Keep in mind that variety also includes the freedom to skip having a family time occasionally. Don't make having family Bible learning times a legalistic ritual that dares not be broken. Share together when you can, but don't feel guilty when you miss.

Involvement. Many family devotional times are unsuccessful because Mom and Dad are the only real participants. Family Bible learning times go best when the entire family is involved. Our family members all take turns leading our family times. Each person, even our five-year-old Bridget, gets a chance. Sometimes the children think up activities of their own. Sometimes they ask for ideas. Whenever they ask for help, my wife or I suggest Scripture portions and activities.

Sharing. Family together times are important because families need times to share joys, problems, needs and prayer. Janet and I find that we are the ones who set the tone for sharing. As children see Mom and Dad open up and tell what is on their hearts, they often have something they want to share too.

Life-linked teaching. As family members share their feelings and ideas there are frequently opportunities for helping children discover the Bible is a practical help for everyday situations.

"I'm scared when the lights are all out at night."

"How can we be kinder to each other at our house?"

"Does Jesus know what I did today?"

Such statements and questions are good springboards for sharing God's promises to be with us and to help us when we ask Him to.

Simple-Fun-Short. As you plan for family time activities, remember that a child usually has a short attention span and is not able to become deeply involved in many adult concepts. If you do not remember this, your children may remind you with restlessness and inattention!

28

Family together times work best if you plan simple activities that are fun and don't last too long. A good motto is: just a few minutes a day will keep boredom away. It is best to end up your family time with everyone feeling a few more minutes would have been fun.

Be sensitive to the mood of the family and gear your family time activity to what is appropriate for the moment. Sometimes at our house we find that a short Scripture and a time of sharing in prayer is just right for our family time.

Relax! We try to make our family times informal, comfortable times. Sit on the floor. Do whatever is needed to provide a comfortable atmosphere. It is important for your family to feel good about what they are doing. A loving, sharing, caring, happy feeling will help your family look forward to your Bible learning activities times.

Alone Times

There is another aspect of good together times that is important. It is the time parents spend alone with each child.

Children need individual teaching because they have special, personal spiritual needs. It helps each child feel secure to know there are times when he can have his parents all to himself with time to talk about what is on his mind.

We have three girls and once each week each girl is allowed to stay up a half hour—or a little longer—past regular bedtime for a cozy time of sharing with Dad. When I have an evening commitment we don't skip our "alone time" but reschedule it for another evening or an available morning or afternoon.

I start our special together time by reading to Heidi or Liesl or Bridget from a book that I borrowed from the library just for her. We then take turns reading from the Bible and we discuss what we have read.

29

Next comes our informal time of talking. I ask if there is anything bothering her or if there is something she would like to talk about. I tell my "alone child" just how special she is to me. We pray and then go to the kitchen for a surprise snack.

Each of the girls seems to really look forward to this time alone with Dad. And they cherish the times they have alone with their mother, too.

I laughingly say I'm not sure whether their time with me is important because of spending it with me or because they get to stay up later or because they like that surprise treat. But I do know that they are wide open to sharing with me and to the Christian teaching that is a real part of our "alone time."

Try to save special corners of time for each of your children every week. A few minutes of individual attention will bring good and lasting results.

Activities for Family Together Times

The following chapters of this book include over 100 family time activities. There are creative art projects, activities to help build good family relationships, Bible games, word games, puzzles, table activities, outdoor activities and just-for-fun suggestions.

These activities can be used anytime—in the morning, after dinner, later in the evening—whenever you can schedule a brief time of sharing together as a family.

We have found in our family that a good time for Bible learning activities is at the dinner table. After the meal is finished we often stay around the table for a game or story, Bible reading and prayer.

Let everyone take turns in leading these family together times. Have whoever is to lead the family time look through the ideas and choose one that he would like to share. Add a circle of prayer and a song and you will have a good time with your family.

Don't feel tied to this material. Adapt the ideas to your own needs. Ask your family for suggestions of things they like to do. Sometimes you may want to just read a Scripture and have prayer. Keep a Bible close by and read a proverb, a psalm or other suitable verse or portion of Scripture. Occasionally have someone share a thought from his personal devotions. Some families might enjoy reading through an entire book of the Bible, several verses at a time. The Gospel of Mark is a good book for family reading.

You will notice that many of the Bible learning activities can be repeated often and still be interesting. You may want to build a group of "core" activities that you use regularly. Some of our core activities are "Sermon Search" (p. 95), "Last Letter Add-a-Word" (p. 74), "Family Question Box" (p. 54), "What About Your Day?" (p. 100), "Give Mom and Dad the Word" (p. 101) and "Silent Devotions Together" (p. 53).

Many times, our after-dinner family times include reading together. We find that reading a chapter from a good book and sharing a thought from the Bible go well together. *Honey for a Child's Heart* by Gladys Hunt, has many suggestions on how to make reading together an enjoyable part of family life.

Look for "natural" family times to share God's Word together. Many family problems such as death, financial difficulties and difficult decisions are natural times for the family to share God's Word and pray together. Special family blessings or occasions can be developed into meaningful sharing times.

During the summer there are many opportunities for

31

outdoor, nature family times. When you go to the mountains, share some thoughts about the magnificence of God's creation or some significant biblical event that happened on a mountain. When you are at a beach, river or lake, take time to discuss a story such as Jesus walking on the water or the foolish man that built his house upon the sand. Take family walks and look for things that are an expression of God's love for us. Look for nature items mentioned in the Bible such as ants, birds, flowers, rainbows, clouds and fish. Then, when you are back home, use a Bible concordance and look up Scriptures that mention these things.

You can also use news events, movies, TV shows and your children's questions and statements as springboards for family sharing. The potential is limitless!

Wherever you are, whether at home or walking in the woods, try to make all Bible learning family times as natural as possible. May I challenge you to share together in God's Word as often as possible? Good times for the family are ahead for all those who will take the step of faith and start including Bible learning activities in the family schedule.

Footnotes

1. Marion Leach Jacobsen, *How to Keep Your Family Together and Still Have Fun.* (Grand Rapids: Zondervan, 1969) p. 19.
2. Gladys Hunt, *Honey for a Child's Heart.* (Grand Rapids: Zondervan, 1969) p. 100.

PART

2

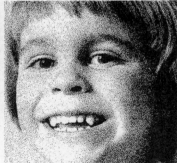

Good Times
for Teaching
Christian Values

Teaching Christian values is not a matter of flipping on a switch at a certain time. If you are involved in the "teaching life-style" described in Deuteronomy 6, the switch will always be on. Every day you will discover opportunities to teach as you live out and talk informally about Christian principles.

You will also want to include planned teaching times when your family studies God's Word together. It is this aspect of teaching Christian values and truths from Scripture that often puzzles parents. Frequently they ask, "What can we do? How can we study the Bible together and not lose the children's interest?"

The following chapters give you over 100 ideas to help you answer those questions.

chapter 3

Good Times with...
Creative Art

In her book *What Is a Family?* Edith Schaeffer talks about the family as *the birthplace of creativity* and she gives suggestions for making creative times in the family meaningful. As your family enjoys the following creative art activities keep in mind these guidelines from Mrs. Schaeffer's book.

"Creativity needs an audience, some appreciation, the response of another human being, as well as the freedom to accomplish, and some raw material to work with. . . .

"Creativity needs the availability of reaching the attention of a sympathetic friend at just the right moment. Someone needs to come and watch, listen, look, *respond.* . . .

"A good rule to remember is that right after the baby song, play or picture has been presented . . . anything you say must be positive. If there is helpful criticism to be given, the first flush of excited completion of a work is not the moment to give it." [1]

Visual Words

Have family members think of a Scripture portion that contains a word which they can print with a visual twist that represents the word. Some visual words are illustrated in Figure A.

Figure A

Have each person read the Scripture and show his word while the rest of the family tells how the visual represents the word.

Crazy Clouds

Read Psalm 97:6. Encourage family members to think of some ways that the heavens show the glory of God. Next give each person a sheet of paper on which to draw clouds. Blue construction paper with white crayons or chalk is ideal.

When everyone has completed his picture, discuss how beautiful clouds can be. Talk about how, with a little imagination, clouds can look like many things (see Fig. B). Have each person take a pen and, using his imagination, create a picture out of his clouds. Share these with one another. Have each family member thank God for showing His glory through the heavens—especially the clouds.

Figure B

Comic Strip Colossal

In Figure C you will find the balloon copy for a comic strip. Make a copy for each family member and have him draw stick figures below each balloon of what he thinks is happening. Show your comic strips to one another. Discuss the different ideas. Then read Colossians 3:12-14. What does this passage have to do with the message of the comic strip? Discuss: Do we always follow God's instructions to forgive one another or are we sometimes like the characters in the comic strip? Why? What can help us be more forgiving?

Figure C

The Dimensions of Christ's Love

Give each family member a sheet of paper and some magic markers or crayons. Have each person make a "picture frame" border on his piece of paper (see Fig. D).

Next, read Ephesians 3:14-19. Have everyone draw a picture of the dimensions of Christ's love. Share your pictures. Discuss: Why does Christ love us so much? How should Christ's love for us affect our love for others? Why?

40

Figure D

Names Are Important

Print in large letters the initials of the first and last names of each family member on a separate sheet of paper. Give each person his sheet and have him draw a picture using his initials as part of the picture as in Figure E.

Share the pictures with one another. Read Ecclesiastes 7:1 and Proverbs 22:1. What does it mean to have a "good name"? Why is a "good name" more important than riches? Think of some people that you know who have "good names." Why do you say that these people have "good names"?

Figure E

41

Have each family member write his first name on his paper and finish the sentence, _____ (own name) is known for _____.

What are some things we can do to help us have even better names? Have each person write on his paper something he will do to help himself have a better name.

Scripture Puzzles

Give each person a piece of construction paper and some marking pens. Have everyone draw a picture of a favorite Bible story or Scripture verse. Next have each person cut his picture into jigsaw-type puzzle pieces. Exchange puzzles and put them together.

When everyone has completed putting his puzzle together, have each family member share a few thoughts about the importance of the Scripture or Bible story represented in the puzzle he assembled.

Love Is Kind

First Corinthians 13:4 says that love is kind. Have each person draw a picture of how this verse is demonstrated in your home. Share your pictures. Ask each family member for ideas on how he wants to be more kind. Have each person secretly decide on one kind deed he wants to do for the family during the week.

Crazy Creeper

Draw a few crazy-looking lines on a sheet of paper. Make such a sheet for each person in the family. Give everyone five minutes to create a picture using the crazy lines in some way (see Fig. F).

After five minutes, share your pictures with each other. Enjoy how creative your family is when it comes to crazy art!

Figure F

Create a Prayer

Gather in a family circle. Talk together and create a prayer of praise that includes the words: *God, beautiful, thank you, people, wonderful, big, small* and any other words your family wants to add.

Continued Story

Explain that each member of the family can help create a continued story. Have one member of the family start and then, after a few sentences, let another family member continue the story. The last person to have a turn concludes the story announcing THE END!

Fingerprint Pictures

For this activity you will need a sheet of paper for each person and one ink pad. Have family members press their fingers, one at a time, on the ink pad and then on their piece of paper. By placing fingerprints on various parts of the paper, interesting designs can be created (see Fig. G).

Notice that no two fingerprints or pictures are alike. Thank God for making each person special.

Figure G

Footnote

1. Edith Schaeffer, *What Is a Family?* (Fleming H. Revell: Old Tappan, NJ, 1975) pp. 61, 62. Used by permission.

chapter 4

Good Times in...
God's Great Outdoors

There is something about being outdoors, close to God's creation that makes it easy and natural to talk about God, His power, His love and His greatness. There can be moments of true family worship as you share thoughts of praise. And there will also be moments that are just right for Bible learning. Jesus often taught outdoors and used illustrations from nature to help people understand His teachings.

The following suggestions for outdoor good times are really just idea starters. You will be able to come up with many other outdoor activities that are just right for your family.

Sunrise Family Exercise

Make this family time a real surprise—and a shocker. Wake up your family early in the morning—at sunrise. Tell them to get dressed because the family is going to have a very special activity. If the weather is nice, go outside and do some calisthenics such as push-ups, jumping jacks, knee bends, etc.

After about five minutes of vigorous exercise, go inside for a hearty breakfast. At the breakfast table, discuss the importance of proper care of the bodies God has given us.

Read 1 Corinthians 6:19. In what ways are our bodies the temple of God? How is it possible to honor God through our bodies? In what way could we apply this Scripture to our habits of exercise, eating, work and cleanliness? Have each family member write down some ways in which he will honor God with his body.

Gossip Gallop

Pluck twenty feathers from a pillow. If you don't have a

feather pillow around the house, you can purchase packages of feathers from a hobby shop. Tell family members that you are going to scatter the feathers around the yard and that they are to collect as many as possible.

The feathers are so light that very few will be found. Use this activity as a kick-off for a discussion about gossip. Discuss: In what way is telling someone a juicy bit of gossip like scattering feathers in the yard and trying to collect them? Read Proverbs 16:28; 13:3; 21:23; 18:8. What are some of the consequences of gossip? What should our attitude be toward gossip? What is one good rule to observe when trying to decide whether or not to repeat something you have heard?

Breakfast with Jesus

Here is another early morning activity. Wake up your family early some morning and take them to the beach, river, or lake for "breakfast with Jesus."

If you are really adventurous, you might want to cook fish at your destination. If not, take a simple breakfast along with you. Before you eat, share the story of how Jesus cooked breakfast for His disciples (John 21:9-14). Talk about how Jesus was never too busy or proud to help others in any way He could. Have family members think of some ways they can show God's love by helping others. Remember that helping people even in small ways can show God's love.

On the way home, let your children stop and share their experience with an older person or shut-in. In this way the family can help someone who is lonely by sharing in a small way—as Jesus did.

Destination Unknown

Plan a secret destination picnic for your family. Say to your children, "Come on, I want you to take a trip with me."

Don't tell them where you are going, only that they need to trust you. When you reach your destination, share with them the story of how Abraham trusted God and went to a destination unknown (read Gen. 12:1-4; Heb. 11:8-10).

Explain that trusting God means doing what He wants us to do even when we are not sure what will happen. God has pleasant surprises for us! Enjoy your picnic.

String Along

Lay out a treasure hunt using a long ball of string. This will work especially well if you can go to a park or empty field with some trees and shrubs. Tie the string to your starting point. Then unravel the ball of string as you lay out an interesting route for your children to follow. Make it as difficult as you think they can handle. At the end of the string, place a nice treat for the searchers.

As they eat the treat, share with them Psalm 27:11. Explain that just as they followed the string and found their reward, so God guides us if we will listen and trust Him. Share that God has given us a map. And that map is the Bible. Within His Word God gives us clear directions for our journey through life. Take a few moments to thank God for His Word and that we can depend on Him to guide us through the difficulties of life.

Pebble Picture

Have each family member find a handful of pebbles. Give each person a sheet of typing paper and have them drop their pebbles, one at a time, onto the paper. Each person makes a dot where each pebble lands, then, using the dots as guides, draws a picture of something in God's creation (see Fig. A). Share the pictures. Thank God for the earth, the mountains, the oceans . . . for the wonders of His creation.

THANK GOD FOR TREES AND BUSHES.

Figure A

Star Gaze

Take the family outside on a clear night to observe the stars. Ask family members to identify stars or groups of stars such as the Big Dipper. Talk about the beauty of the universe and the great God who has put the stars in place.

Read Psalm 8. Ask family members to express their feelings about a God so powerful that He could create billions of stars and yet be so personal that He knows and cares for each one in the family. Have a circle of prayer, thanking God for His power and love.

Water Journey

Water is mentioned in the Bible many times. Have each family member tell his favorite Bible story that mentions water (lakes, rivers, rain, drinking water, etc.). When each person has told his story, surprise your family by taking them for a swim.

God's Gold Mine

Read Psalm 104:24. This verse says the earth is full of God's riches—a gold mine. Give each family member thirty minutes to explore and find nature items to go on a picture. Use moss, bark, rocks, weeds, flowers and such (see Fig. B).

Next give each person a piece of construction paper or other stiff backing, and have them glue these items on the paper making a creative picture using things from "God's Gold Mine." As you make these pictures, talk about the many riches God has given us to enjoy. Share your pictures with one another. Have a circle of prayer with each person thanking God that the earth is full of His riches.

GOD CREATED ALL THINGS.

Figure B

chapter 5

Good Times with...
Bible Learning Activities

The following twenty-one activities will help you plan good Bible learning times with your family. Many families find that after dinner is a practical time for getting the family together for fun and Bible learning. Also, how about Sunday afternoon? Or, some rainy day when the children can't play outdoors? And then, there is summer. Why not plan for regular Bible-learning good times during the summer months?

What's Next?

Read a Bible verse or group of verses. For example, choose a portion from the Sermon on the Mount: Matthew 5,6,7. Begin reading, then stop and have family members try to supply the next word. You might want to give one point for each time a person gives the correct word and see who has the most points at the end of the Scripture.

When the passage has been read, discuss: What was the key word? Why? What did you like most about the Scripture? Why? What did this Scripture say we should do? Was there something you did not understand?

Pantomime Psalm 23

Have family members pantomime Psalm 23. Pantomime is silent acting, using only gestures. When each person has pantomimed, discuss the following: In what way is the Lord our shepherd? What does verse 2 mean? Why should we not fear evil? How is God with us all the time? How can we dwell in the house of the Lord forever?

Silent Devotions Together

Have your personal devotions together for one evening. Have each person read his own Bible silently and have prayer. Children who can't read can look at pictures in their Bible storybooks or draw.

After an appropriate amount of time, give each family member opportunity to share what he feels is the most important point in his Scripture portion.

Do this periodically. It encourages personal devotions and lets children see their parents reading God's Word and praying.

Who Said It?

Following are five famous Bible quotations. Read each quotation aloud and see if the family knows who said it. Find clues by reading Bible references given with each quote.

1. *Where you go, I will go, and where you lodge, I will lodge. Your people shall be my people, and your God, my God* (Ruth 1:16, *NASB*). Answer: Ruth.

2. *As for me, God forbid that I should sin against the Lord in ceasing to pray for you* (1 Sam. 12:23). Answer: Samuel.

3. *For to me to live is Christ, and to die is gain* (Phil. 1:21). Answer: Paul.

4. *Thou art the Christ, the Son of the living God* (Matt. 16:16). Answer: Peter.

5. *Love your neighbor as yourself* (Matt. 22:39, *NASB*). Answer: Jesus.

Have each family member choose their favorite quotation and tell why it is a favorite. What outstanding character quality do you feel each statement indicates? Can the words of these people help us in our Christian life? How?

Practical Proverbs

Before this activity parents should select ten verses from the book of Proverbs to share with the family. Read the verses together and encourage each member of the family to choose one of the ten "proverbs" as his or her favorite. Take turns explaining the meaning of the proverbs. Point out that the proverbs are wise sayings that God inspired King Solomon to write.

Next, discover if your family can write a proverb. Share ideas and write out ideas to see what you can come up with. Here is an example:

A face with a smile lights up a room
But a frown makes everything dark.

Letter your final version on a large sheet of paper. Are there any "King Solomons" at your house?

Family Question Box

Choose a medium-sized box for your family to decorate and use for a Bible question box. Make a slot in the top so family members can drop in their questions (see Fig. A).

Encourage everyone in the family to use the question box to help the family discuss questions about the Bible and Christian living. Periodically, during your family times have a family member draw a question for the family to discuss.

Suggestion: Parents can use the question box to help the family talk about a biblical principle. For example: What ideas can you find in Ephesians 4:32 that will make you a happy person?

Figure A

Add-a-Word

Encourage each person to memorize James 1:19. After reading the verse a few times, say the first word of the verse and have everyone, in turn, add the next word. If a word is missed before the verse has been completed, start over. When you have completed the verse, discuss the following: What does it mean to be quick to hear? Slow to speak? Slow to anger? How could doing these things consistently make our home a happier place to live? What are some ways we can develop these qualities in our lives?

Definitions

(Especially for older children.) Give each family member a slip of paper with a Bible word on it to define. After definitions have been completed (you may need to help the younger ones), have each person, in turn, read his definitions while the rest of the family tries to guess what word he defined. Here are some suggestions of words you can use: *Bible, love, faith, parable, kindness, forgiveness, patience, joy, Saviour.* Have a family discussion on the meaning and significance of each word.

A Time to Be Silent

Read Ecclesiastes 3:7. This verse says there is a time to be silent and a time to speak. Tell the family that for the next few minutes they are to think of what this verse means—in absolute silence. At the end of one minute, there will be "a time to speak." Discuss: What do you think this verse means? When are some of the times God wants us to be silent? When are some of the times that He wants us to speak? Get ideas from Ephesians 4:31,32.

Word Scramble Scavenger Hunt

Divide your family into two teams and give each team the following list.

1. toac—1 Samuel 17:5. 2. kobo—Exodus 24:7. 3. eldnac—Matthew 5:15. 4. rufit—Genesis 1:11. 5. edatrh—Judges 16:12. 6. kebtas—Luke 9:17. 7. saldna—Mark 6:9. 8. wlob—1 Chronicles 28:17. 9. cabhrn—Isaiah 17:6. 10. cokr—Matthew 16:18.

To discover what they are to find, each team must unscramble the ten words on the list by finding them in the Bible references given. (Use *King James Version.*) Then the scavenger hunt starts. Give a big cheer for the team that finds all of the items.

Faith Match

Following is a list of Old Testament men and their acts of faith mentioned in Hebrews 11. Match the men with the act of faith by drawing a line between the two.

56

Abel	Prepared an ark—Hebrews 11:7
Noah	Left Egypt—Hebrews 11:23-27
Abraham	Blessed Jacob—Hebrews 11:20
Isaac	Offered a better sacrifice than Cain—Hebrews 11:4
Moses	Obeyed God by going out—Hebrews 11:8

Next let each family member pantomime the character of his choice. What did all these acts of faith have in common? For a clue, read Hebrews 11:1. Discuss how God wants us to trust Him for end results (read Heb. 11:6). Have each person share a time when they trusted God even when they could not see how things could work out.

Dark Journey

Have the family go into one room of the house while one family member prepares an obstacle course in another room. Place chairs, stools, toys, etc., in the way so it will be very difficult to get through the room. Turn off all the lights in the house and then let each family member, in turn, crawl through the maze. Next, let each person crawl through the room with a flashlight to guide his way.

When everyone has taken a turn, turn on the lights and discuss what happened. How did it feel to crawl through the maze in the dark? Was it difficult? How did you feel when you crawled the second time?

Have someone read Psalm 119:105. In what way is a person in the dark when he does not know God's Word? How is God's Word like a lamp?

Everyone has dark places in his life—places that need the light of God's Word. Have each family member think of an area of his life that needs the light of God's Word. Can anyone suggest a Scripture that will help? Give the family several minutes to talk about how the suggested Scriptures are "lights."

Bible Bumper Stickers

Read 1 Thessalonians 5:12-28. Based on these Scriptures, think up two catchy phrases that would make good bumper stickers. Discuss how these Scriptures can help family members become better witnesses. Write the phrases on strips of paper.

Encourage family members to memorize the phrase of the week and live it out in everyday family situations. Figure B is an example of a possible bumper sticker.

NEVER PAY BACK WRONG FOR WRONG, YOU ALWAYS GET SHORT CHANGED. I THESS. 5:15

Figure B

Sermon on the Mount Slogans

Matthew 5:3-12 contains the Beatitude portions of Jesus' Sermon on the Mount. Read this together, and then make up several slogans based on these Scriptures. Write the slogans on separate sheets of construction paper and display one each week (see Fig. C).

Someone may want to make a stick figure illustration to go along with each slogan. Discuss how these slogans, if lived out, can make your home a happier place to live.

Figure C

God's Escape Hatch

Read 1 Corinthians 10:13. This verse says that God will never allow us to be tempted beyond that which we can endure. He will always provide a way of escape.

In the following situations, discuss what you feel the persons should do and the ways of escape God might provide.

1. John has been severely harassed at school by some of his friends because of his refusal to participate in question-

59

able activities. He is tempted to participate just to get the kids off his back.

2. Mr. Rogers is up for an exceptional promotion that includes a big pay raise. This promotion, however, will mean many more hours a week and a lot of time on the road. Mr. Rogers is tempted to take this promotion because he feels it will put his family on a firm financial footing.

3. Chris is in love with Bob, who is a non-Christian. He has asked her to marry him. She is tempted, but at the same time realizes she might be making a mistake.

Pressing On

Read Philippians 3:12-14. In these verses Paul says that he is not perfect, but that he is growing. God does not expect us to be perfect, but He does expect us to grow toward His likeness. He expects us to press on.

The following chart will help family members "Press on." Have each person make an individual chart as shown in Figure D.

In the left column have family members list areas in which they feel they want to grow. Opposite each area, in the second column, have them write their plan for "pressing on."

NOT PERFECT BUT PRESSING ON	
DEVOTIONAL LIFE 1. 2. 3. 4. 5.	READ BIBLE DAILY PRAY EVERYDAY

Figure D

Discuss-Debate

(Especially for families with teen-agers.) Start this activity by having a family discussion on the common saying, "Most Christians are hypocrites." Tell family members that sometime during the discussion you will have them stop and two persons will be chosen to take opposite views and debate the issue for two minutes.

After the debate, continue the discussion. Here are some questions to stimulate your discussion: What is a hypocrite? Why do non-Christians say that "most Christians are hypocrites"? What should our response be when something like this is said? What are some things we need to be careful of so people will not accuse us of being hypocrites?

Agree or Disagree?

Tell family members that we are going to have an "agree or disagree" activity. Have everyone number from 1 to 5 on a sheet of paper. Explain that as you read each of the five "Agree or Disagree?" statements, they are to write "yes" if they agree with a statement, "no" if they disagree with the statement.

When you have read all of the statements, read each one again. This time have each person raise his hand if he agrees.

Agree or Disagree Statements
1. A real Christian never tells a lie.
2. God always answers prayer the way we want Him to.
3. Sometimes it is all right for a Christian to be unkind.
4. God is interested in everything we do.
5. It is always all right to tell God how you feel, even when you are angry with someone and want to get even.

Discuss each statement. Take time for each family member to tell why he agreed or disagreed.

"Love Is"—Circle Chat

Go around the family circle several times with each person finishing the sentence, "Love is_____."
Have someone read 1 John 3:17,18. You have just talked about love, but this Scripture says that love is *action*. Now go around the family circle again with each person completing the sentence, "I show my love for God by_____ ."

Discuss: Which sentence was the easiest to finish? Why? Have each family member decide on a way he will show God's love to someone else during the next week. Have a "report back" session with everyone sharing how they found opportunities to put God's love into action.

Find Me

Have one person pretend to be a Bible character in some specific location (for example, Adam in the Garden of Eden). The rest of the family must find out who the person is and where that person is located.

Family members, in turn, can either ask a "yes" or "no" question or say "Clue please!" in which case the "hidden character" must give a clue to his identity and location. The one who "finds" the hidden character is the next person to be identified and located.

Magazine Story

Give each family member a magazine. Have everyone choose and cut out pictures that will help him tell a Christian story. When family members are prepared, have them tell their stories, using the pictures they have selected.

chapter 6

Good Times with...
Bible Puzzles

Working together to solve a puzzle can be a time of real learning and lots of fun for everyone involved. Each of the following Bible puzzles is designed to help your family learn Bible facts together. The puzzles will also provide opportunities for family members to build good relationships as you help one another, talk with each other, laugh at your mistakes and join together in reading God's Word.

Find the People

The rectangle, Figure A, contains the names of two famous Bible women. Can you find them by following a regular pattern?

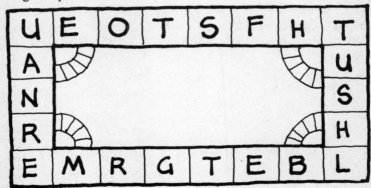

Figure A

The answer is Ruth and Esther. These names can be found by looking at every fourth letter.

Can someone in the family tell the story of these women? (See Ruth 1—4 and Esther 1—9, or an Old Testament Bible storybook.) What outstanding quality did both of these women possess? (Loyalty). Is loyalty a quality that we should possess? To whom should we be loyal? Why? Have each family member ask God to help him be loyal.

Who Lives Here?

An important Bible person lives in each of the houses in Figure B. Can you tell who lives in each house?

Figure B

(The Bible people are: Jesus, Abraham, Stephen, Lydia.)

When everyone in the family has discovered who lives in each of the houses, take turns giving information about each of the Bible people. Use the Bible or a Bible storybook to discover more about each person. What lesson can we learn from each one that will help us live as Christians?

"All About Love" Hidden Word Puzzle

The following hidden word puzzle is all about love (see Fig. C). There are 11 words that talk about love hidden in this puzzle. Some are spelled forward, some backward, some up and down, and some diagonally. Most of these words are taken from 1 Corinthians 13:4-7 in *The Living Bible*. Find the words and circle them.

T	N	E	I	T	A	P	T	M
I	G	D	N	I	K	P	Z	J
F	O	R	E	V	E	R	R	I
R	L	J	E	A	L	O	U	S
T	F	B	U	A	S	U	D	P
L	A	Y	O	L	T	D	E	M
S	U	O	I	V	N	E	T	Q
S	E	L	F	I	S	H	S	A
H	A	U	G	H	T	Y	A	T

Figure C

(The words are: patient, kind, forever, greatest, rude, jealous, loyal, envious, selfish, haughty, proud.)

66

You will notice that some of these words tell what love is and others what love isn't. Assign each family member two words and have him tell what the words say about love. Have a circle of prayer with each family member thanking God for His love. Also ask for help to be more loving to family and friends.

A Cryptogram Message

In a cryptogram message some letters of the alphabet are assigned different meanings. For example, the letter *B* might be changed to *A* making the word *Bible* spelled "Aiale."

A cryptogram rule is that any letter given a new meaning will be used that way consistently throughout the message. To read the Scripture message in Figure D you must discover the letters that have been changed and their new meanings.

CRYPTOGRAM

EUBMIJ   YTURECLVCE   JHCRCFTCR   JT   GTD
RCEIEJ JHC DCVIL,
AND HC WILL FLCC FRTM YTU (James 4:7)

Figure D

Did your family work out the code? Here it is: E = S; T = O; C = E; J = T.

After you have decoded the verse, discuss: What does it mean to submit yourself to God? What are some ways submission can be accomplished? What are some ways we can resist the devil? How did Jesus resist the devil?

Find the Answer

What do the following references say about prayer? What

words can you find to fill in the blank spaces below?

1. Jesus said not to pray like them—read Matthew 6:5.

_ _ _ _ _ _ _ _ _

2. Something Jesus said we are to ask for in our prayers—read Matthew 6:11.

_ _ _ _ _

3. The type of man whose *fervent effectual prayers* avail much—read James 5:16.

_ _ _ _ _ _ _ _ _

4. Something that stopped for three years and six months after Elias prayed—read James 5:17.

_ _ _ _

5. Two words that Jesus prayed in the Garden of Gethsemane which show His attitude toward prayer—read Matthew 26:42.

_ _ _ _ _ _ _

6. Three words that tell us how to pray—read 1 Thessalonians 5:17.

_ _ _ _ _ _ _ _ _ _ _ _ _ _ _ _ _

(Answers: 1. Hypocrites. 2. Bread. 3. Righteous. 4. Rain. 5. Thy will. 6. Pray without ceasing.)

68

Discuss: What attitude should we have when we pray? What was Christ's attitude? What does it mean to "pray without ceasing"? Can this really be done? How?

Crossword Puzzle . . . God Cares

The crossword puzzle (Fig. E) introduces Scriptures for discussion on how God cares for the family. Read the clues aloud and have family members suggest answers to fill in the squares. Make extra copies if you want each person to have his own puzzle.

DOWN

1. What New Testament man, relative of Jesus, said, "You do not have because you do not ask"? (Jas. 4:2, *NASB*).

2. Who performed a miracle and fed 4,000 hungry people? (Matt. 15:32-38).

5. God told Elijah that_____ would bring him food (1 Kings 17:4).

6. Jesus said, "_____, and it shall be given you" (Matt. 7:7).

10. The apostle Paul said that God will supply every_____ of ours (Phil. 4:19).

ACROSS

3. God told Moses to strike a rock so the people could have_____ (Exod. 17:6).

4. God told Moses that He would rain_____ from heaven for the children of Israel to eat (Exod. 16:4).

7. God supplied Jonah with a gourd to give him_____ (Jon. 4:6).

8. Jesus said that the lilies of the field were clothed better than who? (Matt. 6:29).

9. Jesus said that our heavenly Father feeds

69

the_____ and we are more important than they (Matt. 6:26, *NASB*).

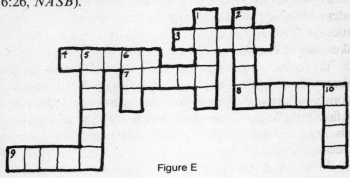

Figure E

(Answers: 1. James; 2. Jesus; 3. Water; 4. Bread; 5. Ravens; 6. Ask; 7. Shade; 8. Solomon; 9. Birds; 10. Need.)

When the puzzle is solved, discuss the various Scriptures: "Why has God given us these examples of how He supplies needs? What can we expect Him to provide for us? What is our part?"

Peacemakers Puzzle

It is sometimes a puzzle to know how to become a peacemaker in a difficult situation, but God's Word helps us put things together in a peaceful way.

Use the Peacemaker Puzzle shown in Figure F to help your family discover peacemaker principles from the Bible.

Working together as a family, follow these steps:

1. On a large sheet of poster board or heavy paper draw a cross and letter "PEACEMAKERS" as shown in the sketch.

2. Draw puzzle sections approximately as shown. In each section, letter the words and Scripture reference as in sketch.

3. Cut puzzle apart and mix the pieces, giving each family member a piece or two.

4. Before putting the puzzle back together, have each person read the reference on his part(s) of the puzzle. Use a modern language version if possible. Talk about how each particular Bible verse can help a person be a better peacemaker.

5. You may want to discuss with your family the peacemaker Bible verses which you particularly need to put into action. Your openness and honesty may encourage others in the family to share their feelings and their peacemaking goals. Pray together for God to help everyone in the family to become a peacemaker.

6. After you have discussed the Bible verses and talked about individual goals, have fun putting the puzzle back together.

Figure F

chapter 7

Good Times with...
Bible Word Games

The Bible word games in this section are designed to be used in families with older children (nine years and older). If you have younger children, include them in the family fun by pairing them with older members of the family. Encourage each pair to work together as a team.

Last Letter Add-a-Word

Have one family member think of a Bible word and say it aloud. The next person thinks of a Bible word that starts with the last letter of the word just said. For example, if the first person said, "Jesus," the next person could say, "Sin," which begins with *S,* the last letter in the word *Jesus.*

Go around the family circle as many times as you like with each person adding a word. When a family member cannot think of a word that begins with the correct letter in a reasonable length of time, he is out of the game.

If you want to make the game more difficult, require that the words be from certain categories such as Bible characters, Bible places, or Bible things.

Bible Word-building Game

Give each family member a sheet of paper with twenty-five squares (see Fig. A). Everyone, in turn, calls a letter. When a letter is called, family members may place the letter anywhere in their twenty-five squares. The idea is to build as many Bible words as possible. Each letter must be used in the order given. Words count in any direction. Give two points for a two-letter word, three for a three-letter word, etc. When the game is over, count the points, and have each person read his words.

Give father five minutes to prepare a short devotional using the words on his card. During the next few days have each family member prepare a devotional using the words on his card.

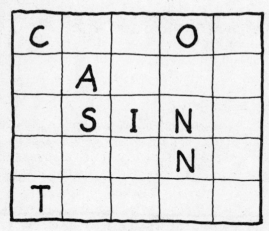

Figure A

ABC Praise List

Read Psalm 113:1 aloud. Tell family members that they will be given fifteen minutes to prepare an ABC praise list. They are to think of something for which to praise God that

75

starts with each letter of the alphabet. Everyone should start with A and continue as far as they can in the allotted time. For example: A—answer to prayer, B—body, C—Christ, D—daylight, etc. See who can go the farthest in fifteen minutes, praising God through the alphabet. Read your lists to one another. Have a circle of prayer with each person praising God. Sing a song of praise.

Abraham Acrostic

Have each family member write the name "Abraham" down the left side of a piece of paper in acrostic form (see Fig. B).

Figure B

Explain that each person is to write sentences about Abraham that begin with each letter in his name. For example, *A* might be "Always trusted God." If family members have trouble thinking of sentences, read the story

76

of Abraham from Genesis 12–25. Also see Hebrews 11:8-10.

Share your acrostics with one another. Discuss Abraham's life. Why was God able to use him to build a nation? What do you admire most about Abraham? In what ways should all Christians be like Abraham?

Fix the Verse

There is something wrong with the words in Figure C. Work together as a family to fix it.

EB ELTNEG DNA YLURT SUOETRUOC OT LLA
(Clue: See Titus 3:2, *TLB*.)

Figure C

When family members have discovered what is wrong (all words are spelled backwards) discuss what the verse means. Have each family member give an example of how a Christian can be "gentle" to others. Why is it important for Christians to be gentle to all people? Is it possible to be courteous at all times? Why or why not? Are we as courteous at home as we should be? Are there some ways we could be more courteous to one another? Why is it important for a Christian to be courteous? Is being gentle and being courteous the same?

Scrambled Promises

God's Word is full of His promises to us. Have each family member think of a key word contained in one of God's promises. Next, have everyone scramble his word—that is, change the letters around. For example, one promise is that all Christians will go to heaven, and the key word is *heaven*. *Heaven* scrambled could look like this: *Venaeh*.

When each person has scrambled his word, exchange papers and let the other person unscramble it. Discuss God's great promises. What would it be like without these promises? What is God's greatest promise? Have each person thank God for the hope He gives us through His promises.

The following references will help your family locate promises in God's Word: Romans 6:23; John 1:12; Psalm 91:15; Psalm 121:4,5; John 3:16; 1 John 1:9.

Hidden Sharp Words

The block of letters in Figure D contains ten hidden words that become "sharp words" when spoken in anger. Find and circle as many as possible. Be on the look out for words that would hurt if spoken angrily.

R	I	D	I	C	U	L	O	U	S
Z	R	A	B	A	D	T	U	M	P
O	F	F	N	T	U	V	S	E	H
T	Q	A	F	O	M	B	C	V	T
L	Z	H	U	L	B	S	M	A	D
W	E	M	G	L	P	O	F	B	W
E	A	D	L	S	T	O	P	C	O
I	S	F	Y	I	S	K	Z	J	R
R	U	H	N	E	V	E	R	O	S
D	P	A	L	K	G	R	N	T	T

Figure D

(The hidden words are: bad, dumb, mad, weird, ugly, never, fault, ridiculous,

Discuss the words you have found and decide:

1. How are these words used sometimes by a person who is angry?

2. How do you feel when someone uses "sharp" words against you? How do you react?

3. Have you ever used any of these words sharply in anger? How do people react when you speak to them angrily?

4. Do you agree or disagree that: *people tend to respond in the same way you speak to them?*

5. What should you do when you are tempted to use sharp words?

Read the following Scriptures aloud looking for prescriptions to help you when you are angry. Proverbs 15:1; 15:18; 16:23; 10:11; 29:11.

Bible Word Scramble

Divide a family into teams of two (a younger person with an older one is good). Give each team a sheet with "scrambled" words from Matthew 7:12, *The Living Bible.* (Sample: For for others them you do what do you to want.) Have teams work together to put words in right order.

After the verse is unscrambled talk about:

1. How do these words from Jesus' Sermon on the Mount help you express appreciation for people in your family?

2. Can you rewrite the verse in your own words beginning: *Appreciate others as . . .*

Scrambled Cities

Following are scrambled names of some Bible cities (see

Fig. E). See if you can unscramble the letters and name the cities. The person who successfully unscrambles a city must then tell one important event that happened in that city.

Cities

MARIASA   _____

MTHBLEHEE _____

RUSELJMAE _____

ROCTINH   _____

MODOS   _____

Figure E

(Cities: Samaria; Bethlehem; Jerusalem; Corinth; Sodom.)

80

chapter 8

Good Times that...
Build Healthy Relationships

"Playing together breaks down the walls that keep people apart," says Marion Leach Jacobsen.[1] And our experiences prove this is true for our family. As we work with our children on a family project or play at some game, we do feel a closeness that is real and good.

The following family activities provide exceptionally good situations for building healthy interpersonal relationships.

Family's Largest Smile

Explain that you are going to have a contest to see who has the family's largest smile. Measure each family member's biggest smile. That is, if the laughing stops long enough! Read Proverbs 16:20. How can a big smile bring joy to people? God? Yourself? What are some reasons that Christians should be happy people? Encourage each family member to smile more and frown less!

Pray for the President

Read 1 Timothy 2:1-3. Does this Scripture mean that God wants us to pray for our country's leaders? Why? Have a circle of prayer with each person asking God to guide our President. Next have everyone write a short note of appreciation to the President. Give him a word of encouragement. Let him know that your family is praying for him. (Your family will probably receive a form letter of reply from the President.)

Getting to Know One Another

Give family members paper and pencils. Have them write each family member's name on the paper and number from 1 to 5 under each name. Say that you are going to ask the same five questions about each family member. They are to write the answers to these questions under each person's name. They will receive one point for each correct answer and a bonus of five points if they answer correctly all five questions on any one person.

Here is how to play the game. Give a family member's name. Ask the five questions given below and then repeat the procedure until everyone has been named.

When you have completed the test, correct the answers. Have each person, in turn, answer the five questions about himself, while the rest of the family corrects their own papers.

Here are the questions:
1. What is his or her favorite color?
2. What is his or her favorite food?
3. What is his or her favorite activity?
4. What is his or her favorite animal?
5. What is his or her favorite Scripture?

Who knew the most about other members of the family? Read 1 John 3:11. What relationship does knowing one another and loving one another have? Why is it important to really know one another?

Ten Commandments for a Happy Family

Have the entire family help write ten commandments for a happy family. Use Scripture whenever possible. (For ideas see 1 Cor. 13:4-7; Col. 3:12-15.) When you have finished the list, write the commandments on poster board, decorate and hang in a prominent place in the house for a reminder of what makes a happy family. Make a real effort to live out those commandments!

Support Your Local Pastor

Pastors need a word of encouragement because they—like everyone else—sometimes become discouraged. Help your pastor feel appreciated by writing a family *thank you* letter to him. Perhaps each family member would like to write a personal note thanking the pastor for some specific thing he has said or done. Read and talk about 1 Thessalonians 5:12,13 before starting the notes or letter.

Poems About Each Other

Write each family member's name on a slip of paper. Put the slips in a bowl and have everyone draw out a name.

Tell family members that they are to write a short poem about the person whose name they drew.

Later, read the poems aloud. Discuss how the poems are different—and how family members are different and unique. Thank God for your family and how God has made each person special.

Have a Good Day

It is important for families to start the day out right. However, if your family is like ours, it doesn't always happen that way.

Have a family discussion on how to have a good day. Discuss the importance of starting the day right. Read Psalm 108:1-4. What does this verse have to say about morning time? Share ideas for guidelines for the family to follow when they get up in the morning. Do your children need a simple schedule to follow? How about a pleasant word for each other? Does the family need to get up a few minutes earlier each day? Could you find time each morning for everyone to have his private devotions? What things usually cause the most conflict?

When you have enough family input on the subject, make a "Good Day List"; that is, guidelines for the family to follow so that the entire family will start the day in an enjoyable way.

Family Communication Guidelines

Does your family have some scriptural guidelines for family communication? If not, have a family time to discuss and adopt some. Here's what you can do. The following Scriptures are all related to communication. Read them together as a family. Then, based on these Scriptures, write five to ten guidelines that everyone feels are necessary for good communication in your family. Post these guidelines in a prominent place in the house.

Scriptures to consider: Proverbs 14:29; 15:1,28; 17:9; 18:13; 20:3; Romans 12:17; 14:13; Ephesians 4:1,2,15,26,32; Philippians 2:1-4; James 1:19; 5:16.

Respect for Authority

Start this family time with a visit to the local police station. Phone in advance and make an appointment. They will be glad to give you a tour of the facilities if they know you are coming.

When you return home, discuss your tour and the meaning of authority. Have each family member tell what he thought was most important about the trip. Read 1 Peter 2:13-17 aloud. What does this verse say about how we should feel about authority? What are some of the authorities each person needs to respect and obey?

Have each person tell what he or she thinks would happen

in your town if all laws were suspended for one day and everyone could do as he pleased without fear of punishment?

Be sure to mention that although law enforcement is necessary, as Christians, we obey not because of fear of punishment, but because of our love of God and others. Discuss: Why does obeying laws show love?

Take a few moments to write a thank you note to the police department for the good work they do in making the city a safe place to live and for the tour of the police station.

What Is a Family?

Give each family member a sheet of paper and a pencil. Have each person complete the sentence: "A family is____ _____." On a clean sheet of paper have each person draw lines to make three columns. At the top of one column letter: *Father;* the next column: *Mother;* the last: *Children.*

Then as a family look up the following verses that talk about responsibilities of family members. Talk together about what you discover. Decide what to write in each column.

Father: Proverbs 19:18; Ephesians 6:4; 1 Timothy 5:8.
Mother: Titus 2:4; Proverbs 1:8; 1 Thessalonians 2:7.
Children: Ephesians 6:1-3; Exodus 20:12.

Discuss: Why is each family member important? What does God expect from each of us?

A Whisper Separates Friends

Go outside to play this game. One person is "it" and tries to tag another person. However, family members may not be tagged if they are holding hands.

A second family member is appointed to be the "whisperer." It is his job to separate the family members holding

86

hands by whispering in one of their ears. When this happens, the two people holding hands must separate and are thus eligible to be tagged by the person who is "it."

After you have played this game for awhile, have someone look up Proverbs 16:28. Discuss: Why is this verse true? Can you think of an illustration of this happening? What precautions can be taken to never allow a whisper to separate friends?

Compliments

Remember that family members should be your best friends. This game builds family friendship. Send one person from the room. Have each person write a compliment about him on a piece of paper.

Recall the person and have a family member read each compliment while the person being complimented tries to guess who made it. Redistribute the sheets of paper and repeat the procedure until each person has been complimented.

Children Are Important

Read aloud Psalm 127 and Mark 10:13-16. Discuss the following questions: In what way are children a gift from God? How do children make parents happy? (Tell ways your children have given you happy experiences.) Why did the disciples try to keep the children away from Jesus? How did Jesus feel about children?

Family Feather Frenzy

Get your family time off to a wild start with a "feather blow." The idea is to work together as a family and keep a feather in the air by blowing. (Note: If you do not have a feather, have the same kind of fun with a "balloon blow.")

Love Helps Families Grow Like Jesus

On a large sheet of poster board or on a long strip of shelf paper letter 1 Corinthians 13:4-7 from *The Living Bible* paraphrase. Read the verses aloud together. Appoint one family member to be the underliner. The rest of the family divides into groups of two or three to look for words they think will enable them to be more helpful to one another. As they decide on words they call them out to be underlined. When the words are underlined, read the Scripture portion together again, especially emphasizing the underlined words.

Footnote

1. Marion Leach Jacobsen, *How to Keep Your Family Together and Still Have Fun.* (Grand Rapids: Zondervan, 1972) p. 14.

chapter 9

Good Times that...
Focus on Values

Do your children know what is really important to you? Do you ever help them understand why you make certain choices?

To effectively communicate Christian values to children we need to share our viewpoint with them, to let them know what is high on our priority list and what the Bible has to say about key issues. All of this gives each child a base from which he can make meaningful choices for himself.

The following activities provide opportunities for parents and children to share feelings and ideas. When we take time to talk about what is important to us—what we prize and what we do—we not only clarify our own values, but we help others to clarify their values as well.[1]

Three Sentences of Jesus

Share with family members that author Philip Wylie once said that he lived his life according to three sentences of Jesus. Give each person a chance to guess what those three sentences were. Here are Jesus' three sentences: *And ye shall know the truth and the truth shall make you free* (John 8:32); *Love one another* (John 15:12); and, *Suffer the little children to come unto me* (Mark 10:14).

Ask family members what they think "living by these sentences" would mean in terms of everyday choices.

Give family members the opportunity to choose three sentences of Jesus they want as guides for living. For ideas see Luke 6:32; Matthew 6:33; Matthew 7:1.

Thomas Jefferson and Work

Share with your family: When Thomas Jefferson evaluated a man concerning his work he asked three questions. 1. Is he honest? 2. Will he work? 3. Is he loyal?

Discuss: What important things (values) are these questions talking about? Discover what God's Word has to say about honesty, willingness to work and loyalty by reading Ephesians 4:25; 2 Thessalonians 3:10 and Proverbs 17:17.

What I Like Best

Have each family member make a list of the five things he likes to do best. Share your lists with one another. Have someone read 1 Corinthians 10:31-33.

Discuss: What does it mean to do everything to the glory of God? Is this possible? Next, have everyone select one item from his list (of things he likes to do best) and tell how he can do that particular thing to the glory of God. Have a circle of silent prayer. Suggest for each person to dedicate each item on his list to the glory of God.

Collect Bible Valuables

Start this activity by having each family member look in his Bible and find five Bible "valuables." These "valuables" can be anything a person thinks is important, such as Jesus, grace, cross, Ten Commandments, heaven, etc.

Give everyone five index cards or slips of paper and have them write a Bible valuable on each card. Together read Mark 12:29,30 and discover what Jesus says is most important. How many "valuables" cards can each person make using these verses?

Next set a waste paper basket against a wall. Designate a starting line from three to seven feet from the basket. Each family member, in turn, tries to throw a ball into the basket.

If he succeeds, he may collect one Bible valuable from each family member. See who can collect the most Bible valuables in fifteen minutes.

What's Most Valuable?

Have each family member write on separate slips of paper what he feels are the two most valuable things in the world. Put all the slips in a container, mix them up and draw them out one at a time. Have family members decide in which order of priority they should be placed. (Recognize that family members will not necessarily agree.) Discuss how knowing Christ influences our choices.

Very Important Things

With your children, look through Christian and secular magazines to find pictures of families having good times reading the Bible, going to church, people helping one another, etc. Together cut and paste pictures to make a "Very Important Things" poster. As you work, talk about thanking God for the Bible, for good times at church and with the family. Say together Bible words from Colossians 1:3: *We give thanks to God.*

Footnote

1. Harmin, Kirschenbaum, Simon, *Clarifying Values Through Subject Matter.* (Minneapolis: Winston Press, Inc. 1973), p. 33.

chapter 10

Good Times with...
Around the Table Activities

A good time for family Bible learning is around the table after a meal. You will find it is easier and more natural to have a family activity when the family is already together than to call everyone from the four corners of the house. Plan for "after dinner" family times by using the following Bible learning activities.

Balloon Night

Purchase ten colorful balloons. On small slips of paper, letter the words to Philippians 4:13 (one word on each piece of paper): *I can do all things through Christ which strengtheneth me.* Insert one word into each balloon and inflate. Make a table centerpiece out of the balloons.

When dinner is over, tell your children that you are going to play a balloon game. Here's how: Each person pops a balloon by sitting on it; finds a slip of paper and places it on the table. Continue this until all balloons are popped.

The family then puts the words of the verse in proper order.

Discuss the following questions: What did the apostle Paul mean when he said, *"I can do all things through Christ which strengtheneth me"*? What are some things that we can do through Christ's strength that we could not do otherwise? How do we receive this strength?

Rhyme in Time

Have one family member create and say the first line of a Bible rhyme. Another family member must complete the second rhyming line before the one who started the rhyme counts slowly to ten.

For example, the first person might say:

Jesus healed the sick,

And the second person might add:

Even some who couldn't kick.

Make sure each person gets a chance to start a rhyme.

Create a Sentence

Have each family member write a sentence using at least 10 of the following 15 words. Additional words may also be used in the sentence. The sentence should be about God's love for us. Words to use: *Jesus, love, trust, peace, care, needs, forgiveness, just, patient, gave, hope, heaven, grace, alone, fear.*

Have each family member read his sentence. Discuss the different ideas. Talk about God's great love for us. What verse in the Bible best describes God's love for us? Praise God for His love!

Sermon Search

This activity can be used many times during the year. In fact, we suggest you use it every Sunday to help your family get more out of the sermon. The following seven activities are for the family to do during the sermon. Assign one or two of these each Sunday. Then sometime on Sunday or Monday (after lunch on Sunday works best for our family) have family members share their completed activities and discuss the message. Here are the activities:

1. Illustrate the sermon with a picture or design.
2. What was the main point of the sermon?

3. What part of the sermon did you like best?
4. The sermon made me feel _____ .
5. I didn't understand _____ .
6. As a Christian I should _____ .

7. Prepare a quiz. Have each family member prepare two questions about the sermon. Collect the questions and have the entire family take the test.

Place Mat Fun

Have each family member write a key phrase from his favorite Scripture verse at the top of a piece of shelf paper cut to place mat size (see Fig. A). Next, encourage everyone to draw a picture of his verse, and decorate the place mat with marking pens or crayons. Have each person show and explain his Bible words and place mat picture. (Help younger children by suggesting a Bible verse.)

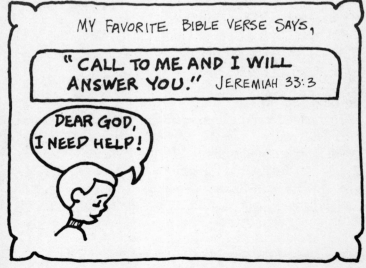

Figure A

96

"God Will Supply" Place Mat

Give each family member a place mat sized piece of white shelf paper and some marking pens. Have each person write at the top of the paper, "God supplies our needs." Each person should decorate his place mat by drawing pictures of things God provides for the family (see Fig. B). Or, the place mat can be decorated with pictures of "things God supplies" cut from magazines.

For additional fun, have each person think of one need that God supplies for the family. Next, scramble (change letters around) the word that tells what he is thinking and write on the place mat the scrambled word.

When the words have been scrambled, have each person, in turn, explain his place mat while the rest of the family tries to unscramble that person's word.

Figure B

"God Is Mightier" Place Mat

Prepare a place mat for each family member. Use a piece

97

of shelf paper, construction paper or even a regular-sized piece of typing paper will do. At the top of each place mat write Psalm 93:4: *The Lord on high is mightier than the noise of many waters, yea, than the mighty waves of the sea.*

Have family members share about times when they have heard the noise of water. Water is so powerful that it is sometimes frightening. It can destroy cities, but also has the capacity to provide power for millions of people. This Scripture says God is mightier than the many waters.

Have each family member draw a picture of some "mighty water" (see Fig. C). As you draw your pictures, discuss God's power. Share your pictures and have a circle of prayer, praising God for His power that created, sustains and saves.

This would be a good place mat to make—when you are at the ocean, river, or near a waterfall. Discuss Psalm 93:4 as you observe the mighty water.

Figure C

Christian Comic Strip

Cut out of your newspaper a comic strip for each member

of the family. Cut off all of the "conversation" and give a comic strip to each person. Have everyone glue his strip on a blank piece of paper and write new conversation copy with a Christian message. Share your "Christian comics" with one another.

King's Business Card

Every Christian is a sales representative in "the King's business." Have each family member design a personal business card advertising his specialty (see Fig. D). Share your completed cards with one another. Discuss 2 Corinthians 5:20. What does it mean to be an "Ambassador for Christ"? What are the dangers? What are the opportunities? Is this verse for everyone?

Figure D

Thoughts

Build a Bible thought for the day around key words like: *salvation, Jesus, Holy Spirit, God's love,* etc. Give family members five minutes to write down all their thoughts about that word. Discuss the word and the thoughts.

Delightful Dinner Time

Have a very special dinner for your family. Prepare favorite foods. Use your best table service. Candlelight will add to the atmosphere. Use this meal to stimulate discussion on how the family can work together to make the dinner hour more delightful. Have family members discuss the meaning of this verse: *Better is a dish of vegetables where love is than a fattened ox and hatred with it* (Prov. 15:17, *NASB*).

Talk about ways the family can make dinner a more pleasant family affair. Include ideas like: 1. Always be ready for dinner. 2. Only positive conversation at dinner. 3. Always say "please" and "thank you" when passing and receiving food. 4. Always thank Mother for preparing the meal. 5. No one leaves the table until the entire family has finished.

You may want to write out your guidelines for everyone in the family to sign showing they want to help make dinner time delightful.

What About Your Day?

Read Proverbs 15:17. Express love at the dinner table by asking about one another's day. Here's an interesting way of doing it. Let each family member, in turn, say another person's name and time of day, such as "Heidi—11:00 A.M." The person being addressed must then respond with a detailed account of what he was doing at that hour. Heidi, for example, might have been in school studying math at the time. She would tell all about her math work. Go around the family circle with each person taking a turn. Make sure each person has a chance to tell about an hour in his day.

100

Give Mom and Dad the Word

Here is another activity that you can do over and over again. An important part of family life is parents sharing memories from the past with their children.

Tell your children that they can think of one word to give each of you. You must then respond with a story from your past built around that word. For example, if the child said to Dad, "barn," then Father must tell a story from his past involving a barn.

Use this activity often. It's fun and will help your children get better acquainted with you and your past.

Secret Cards

Give each family member an index card, pencil and a few minutes of quiet to think and write one specific way he wants to be more like Jesus during the coming week. Each person keeps his own card—a secret between himself and Jesus.

Prescription for Working Together Happily

Read Colossians 3:12-17, then divide the family into teams of two (younger and older together on each team). Have each team take one or two verses of the Colossians passage to read and look for ideas that can help family members work together happily.

After four or five minutes share ideas. Especially talk about verse 17. Can a person wash dishes, scrub a floor, take out the garbage, etc., in the name of the Lord Jesus? Why? Why not? What happens to you and to your job when you tackle it in the name of the Lord Jesus?

Also read Galatians 6:2. Discuss how this Scripture applies to working together as a family. Pray together asking God to help your family discover the joy of working together as a team.

Bible Words Scramble

Have words from Proverbs 15:1 lettered on individual cards (one word on each card as in Fig. E). Place word cards on a table with the first three words in correct order—the other words scrambled. Give your family three minutes to unscramble the words.

When the words are in correct order, read the verse, talk about what it says. Decide on what help the verse gives for how to talk when you are angry. Include in your discussion the idea that we all are angry at times. Anger in itself is not wrong; it's how we handle our anger that counts! (see Eph. 4:26).

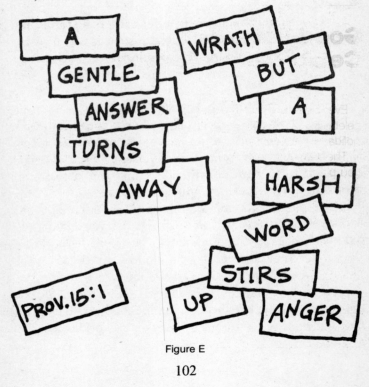

Figure E

chapter 11

Good Times as You...
Celebrate the Seasons

Every season has its holidays that are good times for family celebrations. Why not get a calendar now and start circling holidays that you can use for special family times?

The following seasonal activities will give you ideas to use as you plan.

Sensational Seasons

Each season is given to us by God to enjoy. Start out each season—spring, summer, fall, winter—with a special family time to thank God for the upcoming season. Read Psalm 104:19. Roll a long strip of butcher paper, newsprint, or shelf paper on the floor. Mark off a two-foot section for each family member. Have everyone draw a picture of what he likes best about the season (see Fig. A). Hang the mural on the wall and let each person explain his picture. Decide on some family activities you can do during the season. What are some ways the family can show God appreciation for the beauties of the season?

Figure A

School Days

Each year your children experience some fears as they think about the new school year. What will their teachers be like? Will they be able to do the work? Who will they know in the new class?

To help your children feel better about the new school year, have a "school days family time."

Start by letting each child be the teacher for three minutes. All other family members must obey the teacher. Then have a discussion of your children's feelings. Have each child say what he: 1. likes best about school; 2. likes least about school; 3. fears most about the new school year. Discuss these things. Share memories of your own school days. Read 2 Timothy 1:7 and 1 Peter 5:7. Talk about how God can help us overcome our fears. Have a circle of prayer with each person asking God to help family members who are going to school not to worry, but to depend on Him for help and strength to do well.

End this family time with a fun time by having the children fish for their school supplies. The fish will be: pencils, notebooks, erasers, lunch boxes, etc.

Hang a sheet across a doorway about head height. For a fishing pole, tie a length of string to a yard stick and attach a clothespin to the end of the string. Have one parent behind the sheet to attach the surprises. The other parent should call out each "fisherman's" name. Add excitement by adding some just-for-fun items to the "fish pond."

God's Wish Book

Each year, Sears, Roebuck and Co. publishes a catalog which they refer to as *Sears Wish Book for the Christmas Season*. Why not, this year, publish a wish book of your own? Call it *God's Wish Book for the Christmas Season*.

Give each family member several sheets of paper and marking pens or crayons. Have them "advertise" what they feel are God's wishes for the Christmas season by drawing pictures and creating symbols.

Share your papers with one another and then staple them together with an appropriate cover. Place *God's Wish Book for the Christmas Season* in a prominent place for the Christmas season for a reminder of the real purpose of Christmas.

Halloween Fun and Thoughts

Our family has a tradition that your family might enjoy. Each year, a day or two before Halloween, we carve pumpkins into jack-o-lanterns. Our children then model the costumes that they are going to wear on Halloween. We build a fire in the fireplace, turn out the lights and enjoy the lighted pumpkins as we talk about things associated with Halloween.

One year we talked about fear, another year about what God has to say concerning witches. Another Halloween we talked about masks. We had the children act as if they were really the persons their costumes represented. Then, as we sat in front of the fire, we talked about how people wear masks all year-round. We discussed how some people try to be someone else because they are not happy with themselves or because they want to please their friends. We shared ideas about how important it is for us to be ourselves and not let others influence the way we act (see Rom. 12:2).

We each thanked God for the way He made us and asked Him to help us always be ourselves.

Thanksgiving Frieze

Start this project the first week in November and work on it each week until Thanksgiving. On the first night review the story of the Pilgrims in England and their trip to the new land. You may want to borrow a book about the Pilgrims from the library and read it together.

Next plan a frieze together. A frieze is a series of pictures drawn on a long strip of paper that tells a continuous story (see Fig. B). For paper you may use newsprint, butcher or shelf paper. Mark off four two-foot sections for the pictures.

Ask family member for suggestions of pictures to include on the frieze. For example, you could start the frieze with a picture of the Pilgrims' religious bondage in England. The next picture might be of the Mayflower, the third of the first hard winter and the last, a picture of the first Thanksgiving.

Draw a different scene each week. Display the frieze on a wall in the house. Work on these pictures together. Use these times to express thanks to God for the Pilgrims who valued religious freedom enough to come to this country and risk death for the freedom of worship we now have.

Figure B

Find the Words

Find ten things in the word square (Fig. C) for which Christians are thankful. These words can be found horizontally, vertically and diagonally. Some are spelled from left to right and others from right to left.

```
E  M  O  H  I  R  S  F  F
C  L  O  T  H  E  S  R  R
H  B  I  B  L  E  F  E  I
C  E  P  C  G  E  L  E  E
H  G  A  E  H  R  A  D  N
U  P  O  V  Z  R  M  O  D
R  B  Z  O  E  U  I  M  S
C  A  G  O  D  N  L  S  T
H  T  U  F  O  O  D  Z  T
```

Figure C

(Words you will find are: home, clothes, Bible, food, church, Christ, God, heaven, friends, freedom.)

Discuss the words. What are some other things for which Christians can be thankful?

A Thanksgiving Puzzle Mural

You will need a three- to five-foot section of newsprint or butcher paper. Mark off two large jigsaw-puzzle type sections for each family member (see Fig. D). Put an *X* on one side of each piece and cut pieces apart. Give each person two puzzle sections to decorate with pictures and words. Here are some ideas for things family members might want to include on their sections:

Something for which I am especially thankful this Thanksgiving.

Something for which the Pilgrims were thankful on that first Thanksgiving.

A Pilgrim, a church, a turkey, an Indian.

Something for which I am not thankful but should be.

Illustrate a Scripture verse about giving thanks: (1 Thess. 5:18; Phil. 4:6; Eph. 5:20; Ps. 92:1,2).

When puzzle sections are complete, sprawl on the floor and put the puzzle back together. Tape it together and hang it on the wall. Let each person tell about his pieces of the puzzle. Praise God for His goodness.

Figure D

chapter 12

Good Times with...
Bible Games

What is a game? By combining various definitions we come up with: *game / gām / n: amusement, diversion, a fun activity; usually mental or physical competition conducted according to rules.*

The following collection of Bible games is designed to be fun, and it does include elements of competition. There are also some rules. But, most important, each Bible game provides teaching and learning opportunities for you to enjoy with your family as you play together.

Footsteps of Jesus

Divide the family into two teams.

Goal for Team 1: In ten minutes memorize John 8:12 well enough to say together for the rest of the family.

Goal for Team 2: In ten minutes cut from paper at least six footprints and write on each footprint something Jesus did: loved others; obeyed God; prayed; taught; was kind; helped others; etc. (see Fig. A).

At the end of ten minutes have Team 1 say John 8:12. Then Team 2 uses what is written on each footprint to suggest ways for following Jesus.

Encourage the entire family to talk about what it means to *follow Jesus, not walking in the darkness, but having the light of life* (see John 8:12, *NASB*). Suggest that each family

112

member secretly choose one of the footprints to follow during the week.

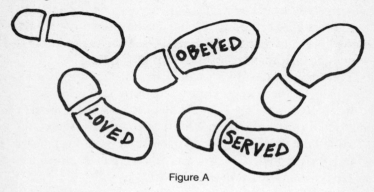

Figure A

Bible Predicament

Have one family member leave the room. While he is gone have others agree on a Bible predicament—for example, Daniel in the lions' den. Bring the person back into the room. He then asks each person, in turn, "What would you do?" Family members should give an honest answer such as, "I would pray a lot." "I would try to climb out."

From the answers given, the one who is "it" tries to guess the Bible predicament. If the predicament is not discovered after the first set of answers, then "it" may ask each family member one more time, "What would you do?" This time everyone must give a different answer.

Give each family member a chance to be "it."

Indoor Olympics

Have an indoor Olympics using the following events:
1. 100-yard dash—eat two saltine crackers and whistle;
2. Javelin throw—throw a straw, then measure the distance;
3. Discuss throw—use a paper plate to toss, then measure;

113

4. Shot-put—use a balloon to toss, then measure; 5. Broad jump—measure each person's smile.

Add some events of your own. Give a first, second and third place for each event. First place receives three points, second place, two, and third place, one. Total the points and crown the champion of your indoor Olympics.

You might want to give handicaps for the smaller children; i.e., let them stand closer, according to their size.

Read 1 Corinthians 9:23-27. Discuss how the Christian life is like running a race. What principles of a successful Christian life does Paul give? (Answer: Desire to win; strict training; clear goal, etc.) How can following these principles help us grow in Christ? In what specific ways?

Spin a Yarn

Take a ball of yarn or string and cut off a five-foot section for each family member. Wrap the pieces around the ball again. Have the family sit in a tight circle on the floor and then say that they are going to spin a yarn.

Start a story about a Christian boy named Randy who is an excellent baseball player. The problem is that his temper gets him into all kinds of trouble. In your family story help Randy find a solution to his problem.

Here's how to spin the yarn. One person starts the story as he slowly unwinds the ball of yarn. He continues to tell the story until he comes to the end of the first five-foot section of yarn or string. He ties the end of his yarn to the beginning of the next piece and hands the ball to the person on his right. That person continues the story the first person started and so on around the family circle until all the sections of yarn have been unwound and tied together. The last person must conclude the story.

When you finish the story, discuss the problem of anger.

What could have caused Randy's anger? What suggestions were given to help him control his anger? What makes you feel angry? What does God's Word have to say about anger? Here are a couple of Scriptures that will help stimulate your discussion: Colossians 3:8; James 1:19.

Newspaper March

Lay newspapers about three feet apart on the floor or outdoors to form a large circle. Tell family members that they are to walk the newspaper circle taking normal sized steps until the leader yells "stop." Then no further steps can be taken. Any person who is not on the newspaper must answer one of the questions that follow. If he answers incorrectly, he is out of the march. If he answers correctly, he may continue the march.

The leader yells "start" and the same procedure is followed until there is only one person left. He is the winner.

Newspaper March Questions:

1. What is the fifth book in the Bible? (Deuteronomy)
2. Who was a brother of Jesus? (James)
3. What does Peter's name mean? (Rock)
4. What was the name of the garden where Adam and Eve lived? (Eden)
5. Ten spies were sent by Moses to look at the promised land. What was the name of one of the spies that brought back a good report? (Caleb or Joshua)
6. What was the second plague that God caused to come upon Egypt? (Plague of frogs)
7. Which of the Ten Commandments contains a promise? (*Honor thy father and thy mother*—Exod. 20:12)
8. What was the name of the famous queen in the Old Testament who risked her life to save her people? (Queen Esther)

115

9. What commandment did Jesus say was the greatest? (*And thou shalt love the Lord thy God with all thy heart—* Mark 12:30)

10. What commandment did Jesus say was second greatest? (*Thou shalt love thy neighbor as thyself—*Mark 12:31)

Card Mix-Up

Before this family time activity, letter each word of Colossians 3:13 on a separate index card. Put word cards in an envelope until needed.

Start family time by having the family read and talk about the meaning of Colossians 3:13. Then, close the Bible and put the mixed-up word cards on the floor. Time the family to see how long it takes to put words of the verse in correct order.

Names in Rhythm

Have family members sit in a circle and start a rhythm by slapping their knees twice, clapping twice and snapping their fingers two times.

The leader gives a Bible category on the finger-snaps. This could be books of the Bible, Bible women, Old Testament heroes, etc. The person on the leader's left must name something in that category on the next finger-snaps.

If that person says an appropriate word, the person on his left then names a new category on the next finger-snaps as everyone continues the same rhythm. Continue this procedure around the circle, until someone misses, then start over.

Bible Art Charades

Divide your family into two teams. Give each team a large piece of paper and magic markers. Have both teams secretly decide on a Bible story or verse to illustrate. At a given signal Team 1 starts drawing an illustration of their verse or story. The other team watches closely, and tries to guess what Team 1 is illustrating.

After Team 2 discovers the verse, it is their turn to draw while Team 1 tries to guess.

When the game is over, have each team share a thought about their Bible verse or story.

The Lost Coin

Mother should lead this family time. Buy ten candy coins. Hide one somewhere in the house. Tell your children that you have lost a valuable coin and you want them to help you find it. After the coin has been found, read together the parable of the lost coin— Luke 15:8-10. Tell family members that you are so happy about finding the lost coin that you are going to divide the remaining nine coins among them. Discuss the parable. What was Jesus trying to teach in this parable? Why is God so happy when one sinner repents? What should our attitude be toward sinners? What is our Christian responsibility toward people who do not know about Jesus? (See Mark 16:15.) In view of these verses, what should we do?

Who Am I?

For each family member make a Bible character card: Noah, Joseph, Peter, Paul, etc. Pin one card on each person's back. Everyone should then try to discover who he is by asking questions of other family members. When everyone has discovered who he is, discuss the various characters. What were they noted for? In what way were they important and what can we learn from them that is helpful for us today?

Bible Professions

Have each family member think of a Bible character's profession such as: Joseph—carpenter; Luke—doctor; Matthew—tax collector; David—king; Paul—tentmaker. Have everyone, in turn, act out a Bible character's profession while the rest of the family tries to guess "who" and "what he is doing."

Correctable Proverbs Collection

All of the following Proverbs have to do with listening to counsel and accepting correction: Proverbs 4:13; 8:10; 10:17; 12:1; 15:5; 18:15; 19:20.

Write each proverb on a separate slip of paper. Cut the slips into thirds. Hide the slips throughout the house and let the family find the pieces and try to make complete proverbs of them. Family members can trade slips of paper. When all the proverbs have been collected and matched, discuss the importance of listening to counsel and accepting correction. Why is it important to listen to counsel of others? Whose counsel should we accept? Why? What should our attitude toward correction be? Why? How can we develop a "teachable spirit"?

Pass It On

Prepare three activity cards by writing one of the following instructions on each of the cards:
1. Pantomime a Bible story.
2. Ask a Bible question.
3. Do something acrobatic.

Have the family sit on the floor in a circle. At a given signal, start the cards around the circle. When the leader calls out "Stop" the persons holding the cards must do what the directions say.

Play the game several times so everyone in the family has an opportunity to participate.

Prepare additional cards using your own ideas. The possibilities are unlimited.

Add-a-Book

Here is a good way for your family to learn and remember the books of the Bible. Have someone start with Genesis, and then continue around the family circle with each person saying the next book until all the books of the Bible have been given in correct order.

Perhaps you will want to begin with just five books. When they have been memorized and everyone is certain about what comes next, then add five more, etc., until all of the books have been memorized.

Secret Bible Object

One family member thinks of an object mentioned in the Bible, such as lamp, robe, rod, rock, fish net, boat, etc.

The other family members must guess what this object is by asking, in turn, the following three questions: Why was it used? Who used it? Where was it used?

The family member who guesses the object is next to be "it."

After playing, discuss: Of all the Bible objects mentioned, which was the most important? Why?

chapter 13

Create Your Own
Bible Learning Activities

Here are basic ideas to help you create Bible learning activities especially for your family. Use the following ideas as "thought starters"; then let your family's imagination and creativity take over.

LEARNING BIBLE VERSES

As your family enjoys family Bible learning activities there will be many times when you want the family to understand a certain Bible verse, to be able to talk about it, remember it and even memorize it. Hiding God's Word in young hearts and minds is easier and more fun when there is a game-like activity to help the memory process.

Mixed-up Scripture Verse

This is a fun and simple way to learn a Scripture verse. Write each word of the verse on a separate 3x5 index card (see Fig. A). Shuffle the cards and lay them out on a table or on the floor. Have the family put them in order. You may want to let each person read the Scripture before attempting this activity.

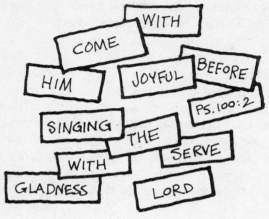

Figure A

Scrambled Words

Key Bible words and concepts can be introduced in this interesting way. Change the letters around in important words and let family members put them in the correct order. Use this activity as a springboard to discuss the words.

For example, you could scramble the following key words contained in 1 Corinthians 13.

Nikd	(Kind)
Tapiten	(Patient)
Sehop	(Hopes)
Eveielbs	(Believes)
Denures	(Endures)

A variation of this is backward words. Just spell the words backwards and see if the family can discover what they are. You might want to introduce a Scripture in the following

123

way. Write the verse on a piece of paper, spelling each word backwards. Give the paper to the family and see who can decipher the verse. For instance, "God is love" would look like this: "Dog si evol."

Add-a-Word

Here is another simple and fun way to learn a Scripture verse. Have family members study a verse for a few minutes and close their Bibles. Say the first word of the verse and go around the family circle, letting each person add a word until the Scripture verse is completed. (You may have to check back to the Bible a few times before you can get all the way through the verse! That's fine.)

Codes

There is something about decoding a secret message that excites children and, I might add, adults. A few ways you can make your Bible learning times exciting by using a secret code are: code a key Scripture verse; code directions for an activity; code questions; code answers to questions.

Make up your own secret family code. (To create a code just substitute a number or symbol for each letter of the alphabet. For example: 1 = A; 2 = B; 3 = C; 4 = D; etc.)

DRAMA ACTIVITIES

As children act out Bible stories, they learn to feel the story and understand more of what happened. As they portray Bible characters, children gain new insights into themselves and others. Make your home drama simple and fun. Remember the purpose is to gain spiritual insights, not to present polished performances.

Some older children will prefer to organize their own plays without any adult guidance. If that is the case, simply give them the Scripture and ask them to plan how they want to act out the story. If they desire assistance, here are some guidelines to follow.

Have your children read the Scripture. Let someone list the characters. Think through the story together. Ask, "What happened first? What happened second? What happened third?" and so on. Discuss how many scenes you will have. Decide who will play the parts. Select some simple props. (A box of Bible-times dress-up clothes will add to the excitement.) Practice the play and you will be ready for a good family time.

After the play ask questions like:

What did you learn from the play? How did_____ (character) feel? What would you have done if you had been in his place? What character did you like best? What did____ (character) do about his problem? How can his example help us work out our problems?

Pantomime

Pantomime is silent acting. Meaning is communicated by gestures and movement without words. There are several ways pantomime can be used as a Bible learning activity. You can read a Bible story while your children act it out. Other times it is fun to let your children pantomime a Bible story or character while the rest of the family tries to guess who or what incident is being pantomimed. Children can pretend they are people in situations such as: one of Jesus' disciples after he sees Jesus is raised from the dead; one of the people who didn't make it into the Ark; Daniel in the lions' den; a missionary; the Good Samaritan.

It is interesting and helpful to pantomime Bible verses like *Be ye kind one to another* (Eph. 4:32), and *Whatever you want others to do for you, do so for them* (Matt. 7:12, *NASB*).

Roleplaying

Roleplaying is a free, informal type of drama where an individual acts out a situation, playing the part of another person. The situation usually involves a problem or conflict. The actors are free to use whatever gestures or conversation they feel appropriate.

Roleplaying is a good way to help children develop skills in solving problems. They also gain a positive attitude about problems as they think through possible solutions to difficult situations. Through roleplaying they are able to experience how other people feel when making difficult decisions.

Here's how it works. Choose a Scripture portion, say Daniel 1. After reading and discussing this Scripture you could initiate roleplaying by describing a typical situation in which children would have to make a difficult choice. You could write it out as in the following example:

Chris and Robert are good friends. Chris wants Robert to explore some old vacant houses that are located near the school. Robert knows that the houses are posted "no trespassing" and that he should go straight home from school. It does sound interesting though.

Let your children play the roles described. Suggest that they act out the roles in their own way. Stop the play before a solution is reached and have the family discuss what they saw and felt.

Ask some questions such as:

How do you think Robert felt? Why did Chris act the way he did? What should Robert have said or done? How do you feel when you have to make a difficult decision? What are some of the hardest choices you have to make?

Puppets

Puppets are an enjoyable way of making biblical and

126

modern-day stories come to life. Your children will enjoy working puppets who represent characters in Bible stories such as Noah, David and Goliath, Moses in the bulrushes and Jesus healing the blind man.

Remember that children are naturally creative and can make up their own puppet shows. Just sit back and enjoy the show!

Puppets can be obtained in several ways. Some stores sell puppets. There are also patterns available from which you can make cloth puppets. (Check with your Bible bookstore.)

Your children can have fun making puppets. Paper-bag puppets are the simplest. Draw the head on the bottom of the bag and position the bottom of the mouth and face where the fold meets the body of the bag. Hair and clothes can be added by coloring or by pasting yarn, cloth or construction paper on the puppet (see Fig. B). Your child should then insert his hand into the paper bag to work the puppet.

Figure B

Cereal boxes make good puppets. You may use a whole box by covering it with paper and drawing a face as shown in Figure C. Another way is to cut the middle front and sides of a cereal box and bend it as shown in Figure D. Cover the box by pasting on paper and adding features.

Figure C   Figure D

ART ACTIVITIES

Art activities are among the best ways to have creative fun while learning important scriptural principles. You don't have to be an artist to enjoy art projects. Children should be our example. They become absorbed in the simplest of art activities. It is only as we grow older that many of us become inhibited and lose our enthusiasm for this type of communication. Each family member should feel that his creation, whatever it is, will be accepted within the family circle. This type of trust will help family members achieve their creative potential.

Through art activities we learn to organize our thoughts and communicate what's inside of us—our feelings, thoughts and knowledge. Here are five basic types of art activities.

128

There are many others. Use the art activities that your family enjoys most.

Pictures

We have found making pictures is always fun. It is especially exciting if you use interesting tools such as magic markers, fluorescent crayons and attractive, easy-to-draw-on paper.

Sometimes we have each family member draw a picture of what impressed him about a Bible story. We then share our creations with one another.

A *collage* is an interesting variation of picture making. It is a creative design or picture which is made by gluing an assortment of things such as cloth, cotton, buttons, beads or paper of all types to a background. Beautiful designs and pictures can be made by this method (see Fig. E).

Figure E

A *montage* is a picture or design made by gluing other pictures and/or words on a background in a creative way. Pictures and words can be cut from magazines, catalogs, newspapers, and greeting cards and then arranged in a design by overlapping the edges and gluing them into place (see Fig. F).

Figure F

Mosaics are pictures or designs created by placing small pieces of construction, tissue or wrapping paper on a sketched picture or plain background. Tear or cut out pieces of paper and glue them in place. Mosaics can also be made from colored rocks, grain, seeds or other such materials (see Fig. G).

130

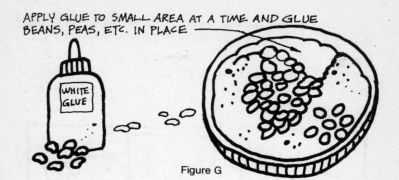

APPLY GLUE TO SMALL AREA AT A TIME AND GLUE BEANS, PEAS, ETC. IN PLACE

WHITE GLUE

Figure G

Posters

Our children always enjoy making posters. A Scripture portion can make a good theme for a poster. After reading the Scripture, give each family member a sheet of poster paper and let him create his own poster. Encourage each person to either draw pictures or cut them out of magazines and glue them to the poster background. Lettering may be cut out and pasted on or drawn directly on the poster paper. Always allow each person time to share his creation. The poster, as with most art creations, can be placed on a wall in your child's room to remind him of the scriptural principle.

Frieze and Mural

A frieze and mural are both pictures drawn on long strips of paper. The frieze, however, is a series of pictures that tells a continuous story. The Easter story, for example, would make a good frieze. Each family member could be given a section of the paper on which to draw his scene. One person could draw Jesus being captured in the garden; another, Jesus before Pilate; another, Jesus being crucified; another, the empty tomb and finally, Jesus with His disciples (see Fig. H).

Figure H

A mural is a single picture that tells a complete story. You can assign various parts of the picture to family members. Draw the mural (or frieze) on shelf paper, butcher paper or roll ends which you can buy from your local newspaper. Cut off the amount of paper you will need and place it on the floor or wall to draw your pictures (see Fig. I).

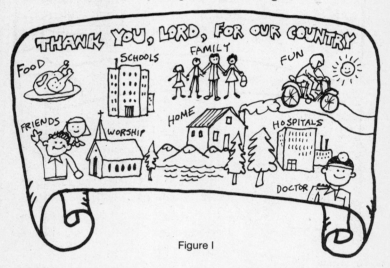

Figure I

Sometimes it is fun to draw individual pictures—to illustrate certain Bible verse—then attach the drawings together to create a mural.

Clay Modeling

Children of all ages enjoy working with clay or dough. A practical recipe for making your own salt/flour dough combines the following ingredients: 1/3 cup of salt, 1/2 cup of flour, 1 teaspoon salad oil and enough water to make a bread dough consistency, probably 1/3 to 1/2 cup. Also add 4-6 drops of oil of wintergreen. Keep dough in a plastic bag in refrigerator. For a larger amount of salt/flour dough, double or triple the recipe.

COMMUNICATION ACTIVITIES

One of the real advantages of having family together times is that they increase communication between family members. Much of the communication during Bible learning activities is in the form of discussion because many of the activities stimulate an exchange of ideas on biblical principles or Bible events. Following are five effective ways to use discussion in your Bible learning times.

Brainstorming

A family brainstorm is where family members throw out a lot of ideas on a particular subject in rapid-fire fashion while someone lists them. After a few minutes of brainstorming, the family evaluates and discusses the ideas. For example, you could brainstorm "ways we can improve our Christian behavior at home." Discuss the ideas and then pick out the top five. Display them for a reminder.

Problem Solving

We should help our children gain skills in problem solving. At times we need to pose problems and then guide their problem-solving procedures. A problem, many times, can be stated in a sentence using "why" or "how." For example, you could ask: "How can we stop criticizing others?"

A procedure for problem solving is:

1. State the problem. (How can we stop criticizing others?)

2. State the facts. (Decide what makes us want to criticize.)

3. Share possible solutions. (Write the list of ways to avoid criticism so that the whole family can see it.)

4. Select the best solution. (Discuss and evaluate each idea before coming to a conclusion.)

Questions and Answers

Questions and answers are a good way to stimulate family discussion. Suppose you were talking about "courage" and your Scripture was about Daniel and the lions' den. You could ask questions such as:

1. What was the king's name who allowed Daniel to be thrown to the lions?

2. How do you think Daniel felt when he was thrown into the pit?

3. How would you have felt?

4. What are some things that make you feel afraid?

5. What can help when we feel afraid?

6. What might have happened if Daniel had bowed down to the foreign god?

Avoid "yes" or "no" questions when possible. Use various types of questions. There are three basic types:

Content (question 1). You ask a content question when you want to know if some facts have been learned.

Probe (questions 2-5). These questions deal with feelings and reasons. They many times ask the question "Why?" or "How?"

Open-ended (question 6). This kind of question allows a person to speculate as to what might have happened.

Open-ended Sentences

An open-ended sentence leaves the completion to some-one else. This encourages family members to share and discuss their feelings with one another. We recently moved into a new house. As we had our first family time we talked about "making a house a home" (see Ps. 127). We used the following open-ended sentences:

1. My home makes me feel _____.
2. When I move to a new house I feel _____.
3. I wish our home could be more _____.
4. A good way to improve our home would be to_____.

After completing the sentences, we discussed one another's feelings about our home.

Sharing

Sharing is an important and effective family activity. Although forms of sharing are used in most of the activities already mentioned, there should be time for spontaneous sharing. This will take many forms. Personal or family needs can be shared with one another. Special answers to prayer and special joys should be shared. Many times a simple question such as "Does someone have something to share?" will open up some stimulating family sharing.

WRITTEN ACTIVITIES

Creative writing is a good way to help children think and express themselves creatively. It is a form of communication which enables a child to reach deeply inside himself and pull out his inner thoughts and feelings. Biblical thoughts, truths, and applications can be shared in this way.

Story Writing

Story writing is probably the simplest kind of creative writing. A story may consist of just a few sentences or many paragraphs depending on the purpose, time available, and ability of the child. For the very young child, creative stories must be dictated to you. The child can tell the story to a parent. The parent writes the story down and then reads it back to the child. When a young child retells a Bible story in his own words, it is a form of creative "writing."

Children need stimulation and input before they can write creatively. For example, say your family is talking about sharing things with others. Then you could write about the boy who shared his lunch with Jesus (John 6:1-14). Before starting to write, help your family think through the story. First read the Scripture and then ask stimulating questions such as:

What do you think the boy looked like? How was he dressed?

Do you think he had friends with him?

How do you think he felt when one of the disciples walked up to him?

Do you think he really wanted to share his lunch?

How do you think he felt after Jesus performed the miracle?

What did he learn about sharing?

Another way to prepare for creative writing is to look at and discuss a picture about the subject. Still another effective way to help the creative writing process is to suggest words to be used in the story. In the story of "The Boy Who Shared His Lunch," you could list words such as *Jesus, boy, friends, hungry, disciples, afraid, miracle, hope, good.*

Open-ended Story

The open-ended story is a form of story writing that is fun to use and encourages creative expression. To construct an open-ended story, write the beginning and let family members write the conclusion. For example, begin a story like this:

The young boy Jude was sitting lazily listening to Jesus tell

137

stories. It was about noon. He was getting hungry, so Jude took out his lunch and was about to take a bite when . . . (finish the story) ———————————————————.

Poem Writing

Poetic expression can be used as an effective teaching tool in the home. We all have a little bit of "Longfellow" in us that, when properly encouraged, can help us express creative thoughts about God. Poem writing can be used to recall Bible stories and various personal experiences, or just to express praise to God.

Poetry can be free verse; that is, non-rhyming, or it may rhyme. Again, as in all creative writing, children can be stimulated by hearing or reading Scripture or Bible stories, studying pictures, taking a nature walk, or looking at and studying a list of carefully selected words on a particular subject.

If in your family time you are talking about God's creation, take a nature walk in your neighborhood. Have each person look at God's handiwork in nature and write down the things he likes best.

Then, when you return home, discuss what you have seen and let each person create a poem. A child's poem from such an experience would be quite simple, such as:

Today I went for a walk
I saw a rose, a squirrel and a tree
They were very beautiful
And God made them just for me:

Paraphrase

Bible paraphrase is putting Bible verses into our own words. This activity can enable parents to help children with

138

difficult Bible words and concepts. Also, paraphrasing helps each person understand what a Scripture portion is saying. If you are talking about John 3:16, give each person a piece of paper and pencil and tell him to rewrite the verse using his own words (see Fig. J). Sometimes your children will need you to help them define or think of an appropriate word. Help only when they ask or you think it is necessary. Your child's finished product might look like this:

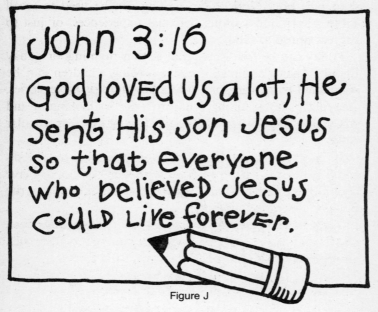

John 3:16
God loved us a lot, He sent His son Jesus so that everyone who believed Jesus could live forever.

Figure J

When your paraphrase project is finished, let each person share his verse. Many times this will stimulate further discussion and deeper understanding of the verse.

Adolescents and adults will enjoy the challenge of paraphrasing the Scripture without using any of the words in the original text.

chapter 14

Now It's Time to Plan

Good times in the family do not happen unless we plan for them. Lack of planning, not lack of good intentions, is the biggest hindrance to good family times. With the incredible pressure of a busy society, parents need to consciously plan for family times and to build them into the family schedule.

This last chapter of *Good Times for Your Family* is designed to help you, the parent, evaluate your family's needs and to help you plan for ways and times that you can have good Bible learning times in your family.

My phone rang. A troubled dad said, "Can you come over—right now?"

Moments later, the grief-stricken Christian father poured out his heart. His son had been caught with dope in his possession.

"Where have we gone wrong? We have tried to raise him to know right from wrong. I just can't understand it."

Further conversation revealed that although the boy's parents were Christians there had been little Bible teaching in the home and few times when the family had planned together times. Everyone was busy. Everyone more or less took it for granted that they had a "Christian family."

Let's look at another family.

The father is a retired military officer—a former U2 pilot. A short time after he accepted Christ he decided to take Deuteronomy seriously and shoulder the responsibility for biblical instruction in the home. Following God's instructions the family started having Bible study times together. The father was also convinced that each child needed individual attention and teaching, so he scheduled some time each week with each of the five children.

What has been the result of this family-centered Christian education? Turned-off kids? Bitter? Resentful? Not at all! In fact, just the opposite is true.

The youth minister of the church where this family attends recently told me, "When there are new Christians in the youth group who need Christian teaching, I turn them over to Ward's kids. They're the best disciplers I have."

What a testimony to the results of doing things God's way! Out of this home have come teen-agers who not only have a strong faith themselves, but also the knowledge, commitment and love to teach other youth their own age.

Somewhere between these two families, however, lies the average Christian home. No really big problems with the kids. Just the normal frustrations of raising children. But at the same time no planned Bible teaching within the home. Very few, if any, good family times around God's Word. This doesn't need to be how it is with your family!

The following pages are designed to help you evaluate the different ways you are communicating Christian values and biblical truths in your family at the present time. There are also planning guides to help you look ahead and think through your goals as you plan for family times and family Bible learning activities.

Before You Begin to Plan

Before you start evaluating and planning take time to think again about what the Bible says concerning the importance of family-centered teaching.

143

As I mentioned in Chapter 1, one of the clearest family concepts in the Bible is that parents are primarily responsible to teach Christian values to their children.

The writer of Deuteronomy gives parents a plan for home-centered teaching:

And you shall love the Lord your God with all your heart and with all your soul and with all your might. And these words, which I am commanding you today, shall be on your heart; and you shall teach them diligently to your sons and shall talk of them when you sit in your house and when you walk by the way and when you lie down and when you rise up. When your son asks you in time to come, saying, "What do the testimonies and the statutes and the judgments mean which the Lord commanded you?" then you shall say to your son . . . (Deut. 6:5-7,20,21, *NASB*).

This Scripture gives the three basic types of teaching in which parents need to be skillful:

• Modeling: *And these words, which I am commanding you today, shall be on your heart.*

• Formal instruction: *And you shall teach them diligently to your sons . . .*

• Informal instruction: *And shall talk of them when you sit in your house and when you walk by the way and when you lie down and when you rise up . . . when your son asks . . . then shall you say . . .*

When you keep each of these three aspects in mind it helps us evaluate what teaching and learning is going on in our homes.

The following pages are designed to help you evaluate the different ways you are communicating Christian values in your family. There are also planning guides to help you think through the goals that you have for your family together times.

144

Modeling (Teaching by Example)

We are teaching our children the following Christian qualities and values by our example in everyday living.

1.

2.

3.

4.

5.

We are teaching our children the following *non*-Christian qualities and values by our example in everyday situations.

1.

2.

3.

4.

5.

We will ask God for His help in changing the following areas of our lives so that we will be better Christian examples for our children.

1.

2.

3.

4.

5.

Teaching Diligently (Formal Teaching)

We could usually have the family together for a family Bible sharing time at:

First choice

Alternate choice

Three good books that we could read and share together are:

1.

2.

3.

The best time for us to have "alone times" with each of the children would be:

Child 1

Child 2

Child 3

Child 4

Talk (Informal Teaching)

During the last week we have used the following situations to help us talk about a scriptural truth.

1.

2.

3.

During the last week we have not used the following situations to talk about God and His Word although they would have been good opportunities to do so.

1.

2.

3.

Setting Personal Goals

We especially want to communicate the following five Christian values to our children. (Note: Values are those concepts and principles that you feel are most important as guides for your life. You might choose things like: love for God—a top priority; God's Word as a guide for life; patience; self-control; diligence—sticking to a task.)

1.

2.

3.

4.

5.

We feel the following Scriptures encourage us to communicate these values to our children.

1.

2.

3.

4.

5.

Here are specific ways we feel that we can effectively teach something about these values to our children. (Avoid general ideas. List specific activities and plans.)

1.

2.

3.

4.

5.

These are our personal goals for putting these five values to work in our own lives.

1.

2.

3.

4.

5.

Goals for Bible Learning Times

As we share Bible learning times within our family, here are some of the special goals we have for communicating God's truth to each of our children.

Child 1

Goal 1

Goal 2

Goal 3

Child 2

Goal 1

Goal 2

Goal 3

Child 3

Goal 1

Goal 2

Goal 3

Child 4

Goal 1

Goal 2

Goal 3

The Challenge: Generation after Generation

When you plan for family times around God's Word, you are not only building patterns of Bible learning for your own home, but also for future homes. Gladys Hunt tells the story of how her grandfather insisted on daily family Bible reading—three times a day. After telling this to some young couples and describing how her father had followed the same pattern, she was asked by one young father, "Didn't you all grow up resenting your father and Christianity?"

Her answer has implications for every Christian family. "Quite the other way around. In all honesty, our parents and memories of our family life are extra dear because of this. Four new families have come out of our parental home, involving fourteen children from four to twenty-two and each family follows the patterns that we learned at home. Our expectations are that each of these fourteen will pursue a similar practice in their homes in years to come."[1]

Don't wait! Today is a good day to start including Bible learning times in your family's schedule. You can expect your children to value and enjoy your times around God's Word when they are good times of fun and warm family sharing.

Footnote

1. Gladys Hunt, *Honey for a Child's Heart.* (Grand Rapids: Zondervan, 1969) p. 92.